resistance

Also by Tori Amos

Tori Amos: Piece by Piece (written with Ann Powers)

tori amos

resistance

A SONGWRITER'S STORY OF HOPE, CHANGE, AND COURAGE

ATRIA BOOKS

New York London Toronto Sydney New Delhi

ATRIA
BOOKS

An Imprint of Simon & Schuster, Inc.
1230 Avenue of the Americas
New York, NY 10020

First Atria Books hardcover edition May 2020

ATRIA BOOKS and colophon are trademarks of Simon & Schuster, Inc.

For information about special discounts for bulk purchases, please contact Simon & Schuster Special Sales at 1-866-506-1949 or business@simonandschuster.com.

The Simon & Schuster Speakers Bureau can bring authors to your live event. For more information, or to book an event, contact the Simon & Schuster Speakers Bureau at 1-866-248-3049 or visit our website at www.simonspeakers.com.

Interior design by Jason Snyder

Manufactured in the United States of America

10 9 8 7 6 5 4 3 2 1

Library of Congress Cataloging-in-Publication Data has been applied for.

ISBN 978-1-9821-0415-3
ISBN 978-1-9821-0417-7 (ebook)

For Mary Ellen Copeland Amos
1929–2019

resistance

introduction

I HAVE A SCULPTURE in my New York apartment called *Defiance*. It's of a woman; she's turquoise, and her hair is flying.

Being in opposition to something is to be in a position of power. It's not simply reactionary. Defiance can be active and can be the genesis of something. You don't want to play the victim. You want to have conviction.

Because make no mistake: we are living in a moment of crisis. Of unprecedented crises.

It seems that in every possible sphere, we are all confronting dark forces that aim to divide us as a world, as countries, as people, as artists, as creators. It's not just the political sphere—everything has become inherently political. From the Oval Office, Parliament, and the Kremlin to recording studios and the labels that staff them, to schools and conservatories, city halls and main streets, the oceans and their shores, we are seeing how those who wish to control us are all too happy to take advantage of any opportunity that would diminish our goals of liberty, freedom, artistic expression, and conservation of nature.

As someone who has been in the music industry for the better part of forty years, who has traveled to and performed for varied and diverse audiences, I have had the privilege of hearing the stories of people from all over the world, and this perspective has given me a sense of how dire things have become. But it has also given me a stronger sense of resistance, of fighting back, of how we might find deep within ourselves the capacity not just for resilience but for healing and for emerging victorious from this most trying of times. And it has illuminated to me how vital the role of the artist is within a society. It has, in a way, revealed to me how hallowed the space an artist inhabits truly is—and how crucial it is that we protect that space with intelligence and passion.

What follows in this book is my journey to engage, examine, and then reassess the artist's role in society and, by doing so, to create a way forward for us as we commit to resist those dark forces that would wish to subjugate us instead of lifting us up and giving a voice to the best in us. It is a mission to reckon with how the current moment is truly one of *Now or Never*. It is a mission to recognize the power of the Muses and the strongest of our creative impulses so that we may transform this moment of crisis into a future of promise.

Join me on the path of resistance—of the art that will set us free.

GOLD DUST

Sights and Sounds
pull me back down another year
I WAS HERE
I WAS HERE
Whipping past
the reflecting pool
me and you
skipping school

and we make it up
as we go along
we make it up as we go along

You said—
you raced from Langley—
pulling me underneath
a Cherry Blossom
canopy
—DO I HAVE—
of course I have,
beneath my raincoat,
I have your photographs.
and the sun on your face
I'm freezing that frame

{ { {

and somewhere Alfie cries
and says
"Enjoy his every smile
you can see in the dark
through the eyes of Laura Mars"
—How did it go so fast—
you'll say
as we are looking back
and then we'll
understand
we held Gold Dust in our hands

Sights and Sounds
pull me back down another year
I WAS HERE
I WAS HERE
Gaslights
glow in the street
Twilight held us
in her palm
as we walked along

and we make it up
as we go along
we make it up as we go along

〉 〉 〉

letting names
hang in the air
what color hair
Autumn knowingly
stared
and the day that
she came
I'm freezing that frame
I'm freezing
that frame

and somewhere Alfie smiles
and says
"Enjoy her every cry
you can see in the dark
through the eyes of Laura Mars"
—how did it go so fast—
You'll say
as we are looking back
and then we'll understand
we held Gold Dust
in our hands
in our hands
in our hands

"*GOLD DUST*" *USUALLY TRANSPORTS* me to Washington, D.C. The song references different decades:

The '60s, when *Alfie* the film was released; the decade I was born in.

The '70s, when I was skipping school and playing piano in D.C. bars and congressional parties during a Democratic administration.

The '80s, when I was still playing piano bars but now three blocks from the White House during a Republican administration.

The '90s through to the present, with the song revealing different snapshots of time as I played concerts in D.C. through two administrations, during peacetime and wartime.

"Gold Dust" began when I was pregnant with my daughter, Tash, in the year 2000. The song was written about twenty years after I was in my teens, a time when I was evolving from a girl into a young woman playing hotel lounges a few blocks from the White House. But it took eighteen years after the song was written, on Tash's eighteenth birthday, for me to really see the many snapshots tethered to it—and what they want to activate in my life right now.

Before my eyes in real time, as I watched Tash emerge as a young woman, the memories of the day eighteen years before became very clear. It had been a tough couple of months leading up to that day in September 2000. Because of medical issues I was having, we were advised to leave our home in Florida and relocate to D.C. for a few months. As I had a high-risk pregnancy, I had to respect the doctor's opinion. So the seeds for "Gold Dust" were planted before Tash and I had even left our home. To get us from Florida to D.C., the song acted as a portal, and my teenage self became my guide.

She took my hand, and as we walked through the streets of Georgetown by the Potomac River, as we passed the Lincoln Memorial on our way to see the doctors, she said, *We were here. . . . You might not remember all that happened here, all that we heard and all that we observed. And that's okay. You are worried about the birth of your daughter. I can't imagine. But this place will feel more familiar once I've reminded you of that time.*

Over the years I have run into my teenage guide—usually when there is a "How did we get here?" moment—and the answer from the Muses is always the same: *Follow the threads that are woven within the Song Beings. They will get you to where you need to go. And be receptive to which Song Beings are coming to you, not just the ones you personally favor.*

"Gold Dust" is taking me back in time again, my teenage self guiding me as I write this.

1977

When I was thirteen, a couple of months shy of my fourteenth birthday, my father took me to Georgetown to get a professional job playing piano and singing. It's a fact that my father, the Reverend Edison McKinley Amos, soon to be the Rev. Dr. E. M. Amos, had more than a dose of Mama Rose (the most infamous stage mother of all time) pulsing through his veins.

And although he was a man of the cloth, he was also a tenaciously pragmatic force to be reckoned with, especially if you were his teenage daughter. I'll never forget his summation of my life as the two of us drove to Georgetown that balmy afternoon. With my mother visiting relatives in North Carolina and my two older siblings having fled the nest, it really was just the two of us on this penitent road to achieve, as the good reverend revealed, my salvation.

{ { {

The sermon began as we pulled out of the parsonage's driveway in the shadow of the Good Shepherd United Methodist Church, my father being the appointed shepherd to that flock since 1972. The personally directed sermon went something like this . . .

Myra Ellen, like Jonah in the Old Testament you refused to fulfill
God's divine plan which had been bestowed upon you since you

were two and a half years old. You were entrusted with the gift of music before you could talk. Being the youngest musician accepted into the Peabody Conservatory at five years of age the trajectory was clear. God had shown me a vision of you playing on a concert stage by the time you were thirteen. But like Jonah you turned your back on the mission that God had assigned for you. Because of your rebelliousness toward your professors and your disrespect for classical and sacred music with that sassy attitude—you got yourself kicked out of the conservatory at eleven years of age. The way I see it you are drowning in your own self-destructive sea of mediocrity. After betraying God and drowning as well, Jonah spent three days inside of a whale. You have spent three years of ignoring your potential. So God has directed me to take you to Georgetown where he will guide us to a place for you to play music and learn your craft. It may be a smaller stage than you could have been playing, but God will provide.

Together with me dressed in my sister's clothes and platform shoes and my father declaring his faith with his clerical collar secure above the cross pinned to his lapel, we asked to play at every restaurant and bar on M Street. Following many hours of rejections, and after the sun had set, I finally said, "Look, thanks for trying, Dad, but obviously there is no room at the inn for us, so can we just go home? We don't have to tell anybody about this." With a pained but determined look in his eyes he said, "Elly, my God will not fail us." At what seemed to be the last remaining bar in Georgetown, Mr. Henry's on Wisconsin Avenue, my father spoke with a tough-looking guy standing by the door. The guy told us to wait while he got the manager. Once my father explained that he was hoping to find a place where I could play, the manager agreed to let me try. If I was any good, I could play for tips.

The bar had only male customers. After I had played a song on the upright piano, the men started making requests and putting dollars in a brandy snifter that someone had put on the piano. The requests were for popular songs of the day, with a nod to show tunes. When I did not know a song, I would write the title down and promise that if I was invited back next weekend, I would learn it and play it for the customer if he came back to see me. After I had gotten my bearings, I glanced over at my dad. The clerical collar was an icebreaker because at first the customers assumed he was wearing a costume. Once it had rippled through the room that he was an actual preacher and I the daughter of a preacher man, curiosity about our plight and then advice to us began in earnest. Some of the customers looked like lumberjacks, others like John Travolta in *Saturday Night Fever*, and then some of them looked like deacons in a church or congressmen you'd see on TV. After I had played for several hours, my dad and I were happy to be invited back to play the following Friday night.

We did not experience Mr. Henry's as "a den filled with deviants," as defined by some of my father's parishioners. Once they found out about the gay bar that had given me a chance, some good Christians warned that we along with those homosexuals were going to burn in the fiery rivers of hell. I was quite proud of my father's response to that rabble: "There is no safer place for a thirteen-year-old-girl than in an all-gay bar." Amen, Dad.

DEVILS AND GODS

Devils and Gods
now that's an idea
But if we believe
that it's they who decide
that's the ultimate
detractor of crime
'cause Devils and Gods
they are you and I
Devils and Gods
they are you and I
Devils and Gods
safe and inside

1979–1980

The clientele changed.

My role as happy hour pianist was to underscore the liquid hand-shake. Management made it very clear to me that my job was *not* to distract our working customers. The lounge was an extension of the office; it was not a place for the chanteuse to sing her evening set and help the customer feel a little less lonely. That would happen in the after-hours set list, when the volume on the small amplifier could be boosted and the job was to entertain and keep the customers company while they had their nightcap.

But at happy hour, deals were being forged, and even though I was not aware of the details, I was a witness to something dark occurring. A witness to a war of ideas being waged. Somewhere be-tween requests for "As Time Goes By" and "Mean to Me," a segue into "Send in the Clowns," then "Don't Cry for Me, Argentina" to "My Way," strategic moves were being played by political opera-tives, by lobbyists and consultants for Big Corp and Big Oil and by bankers who expected a return on their investment in a politician.

Then, of course, there were the intellectuals, who were easy to spot. Some were being hired by the power and money behind the think tanks and foundations that were popping up faster than fire ant colonies in Florida. War rooms, disguised as offices, were being carved out on and around the K Street corridor. But the establishments for which I played forbade the staff from challenging the customers' opinions. The maître d's would warn us that the managers kept their eyes open for any rebels in the ranks.

No one would laugh or bat an eye when the piano piped up through billowing cigarettes and cigars with "Smoke Gets in Your Eyes." *Don't worry, sir: I am not saying a word about Big Oil to any of our patrons.*

But teenagers will be teenagers. And during the late afternoon service, when I was required to play music that would not disturb the dealmakers, playing a variation on a theme of "Last Chance Texaco" by Rickie Lee Jones was irresistible. (No one was the wiser. I knew my crowd.) This was a song that might not have been reactionary when Jones released it in 1976, but songs can take on a meaning of their own, and this was my quiet protest, underscoring the champagne toasts made by the lobbyists for Big Oil.

During this time delicate political discussions were under way that involved some of the country's most pressing cultural conflicts. By the time I was seventeen, I was playing in a hotbed of conservative thinking on its rise to power.

One of my bosses once said to me, "This scene is as sexy as it gets."

But everybody just looked old to me. "All I can smell is smoke," I replied.

And he said, "All I can smell is money."

The young artist's journey is made up of a number of components, not least the ways they see older people act when it comes to issues of morality and accountability. It was no coincidence that a father like mine—who had bucked Christian conventions that would have stopped me entertaining a gay clientele, conventions that would have stopped me from sharing my piano playing with a diverse crowd of patrons—would lead me to a job from which I could observe the interactions of people of great influence.

Just as a gay bar may have been the safest place for a thirteen-year-old girl, a hotel bar near the White House was the most revealing place for a teenage girl to bear witness to the wheeling and dealing of supposedly moral men, some of whom were laying the groundwork for a compromised future.

LITTLE EARTHQUAKES

Yellow Bird flying get shot in the wing
good year for hunters and Christmas parties
and I hate
and I hate
and I hate
elevator music
the way we fight
the way I'm left here silent
oh these little earthquakes
here we go again
these little earthquakes
doesn't take much to rip us into pieces

we danced in graveyards with vampires till dawn
we laughed in the faces of kings never afraid to burn
and I hate
and I hate
and I hate
disintegration
watching us wither
black winged roses that safely changed their color

ζ ζ ζ

I can't reach you
though I feel you in my head
I can't reach you
though I know you're in my head
I can't reach you
I can't
reach
you
give me life give me pain give me myself again
give me life give me pain give me myself again
give me life give me pain give me myself again
give me life give me pain give me myself again
these little earthquakes
here we go again
these little earthquakes
doesn't take much to rip us into pieces

FOR A LONG TIME, I didn't appreciate that for certain songs to show themselves to me, they have to trust that I am ready to carry them. Some songs require a willingness from me to research the subject that makes up their core. Others will work with me only if I have personally experienced the emotion they are investigating. The weight of processing conflict can be off the scale. The wounds can run deep—and they most certainly did during the writing of "Little Earthquakes."

I have played this song on many concert tours in response to conflicts and to look at my part in those conflicts or my reaction to them, no matter how painful. Conflict brings up so many emotions—some that may have been hiding in my blind spot. These feelings can be challenging to confront.

Over the years "Little Earthquakes" has been called upon to work through collective trauma. During 2017 she was requested during my Native Invader tour in order to help process the shock of a Trump presidency. After all, there are moments in history that intersect with us, and sometimes it is hard to gauge how these moments will translate down the line and how they will reverberate in our lives.

Then there are precipitating events that can be seismic in effect.

{ { {

People I thought I had known changed before my eyes from November 4, 1979, through January 20, 1981. The images of blindfolded Americans being held hostage in Tehran, Iran, shook the foundations of the nation.

Initially there was an outpouring of American public support for Jimmy Carter. My father would say, "Jimmy Carter got my vote and will do so again no matter what I have to put up with because his heart is in the right place and he is a good guy." However, the opinion on what skill set a president needs to lead a nation in crisis can change, and the emotional tone of a nation can change. With the TV acting as our daily emotional conductor, a national obsession with the American hostages began to happen soon after they were taken. They had been taken with the seizure of the American embassy in Tehran on November 4, 1979, by students calling themselves Muslim Student Followers of the Imam's Line.

The students were supporters of the Ayatollah Khomeini, one of the leading imams of the Iranian Islamic Revolution. Earlier that year, in January, these students were gaining momentum with the overthrow and subsequent exile of the shah of Iran—head of the pro-Western, authoritative, Persian monarchy, backed by the United States.

Leading up to the capture of the American hostages, the students had demanded the return of the shah to stand trial for crimes against his people. For decades the shah of Iran's brutal secret police, SAVAK, silenced thousands of opponents and critics of the shah by hunting them down and executing them.

By October 1979 Jimmy Carter was in an impossible situation.

For months friends of the shah, including prominent Republicans, some Democrats, and Big Corp allies, were putting huge pressure on the Carter administration to allow the shah a safe haven in America. Once it was known the shah needed treatment for cancer, the pressure grew, some saying it was a disgrace not to let him in. Although someone from the State Department made a list of *horrible things* that could happen if they did. Did Carter voice his fears, asking those pressuring him, If the Iranians react negatively, if they should seize our State Department officials there and make them hostages, then what is your policy? Was the response dead silence?

But then Carter buckled. On October 22 the deposed shah was given asylum to get medical treatment in New York. The Ayatollah Khomeini responded, "The United States, which has given refuge to that corrupt germ, will be confronted in a different manner by us."

The American hostages' horrible plight became an extension of our daily lives. Four days after the Americans were taken, ABC began broadcasting a late-night series called *America Held Hostage: The Iran Crisis*. As days turned into weeks turned into months, in newspapers and nightly news accounts the country learned about the individuals being held hostage and their families. The questions were unrelenting: *How long can they last without suffering long-term mental and physical damage? Are they being tortured?* It became clear that people saw the hostages as an extension of themselves.

Every night people from all around the country would see the burning of the American flag and hear chants of "Death to America!" or screams of "Den of Spies!" coming from the occupied American embassy. People were using a new term to describe their reactions to this: "IRAGE." The effect of these images on our country—a country that had been allergic to military intervention after the loss of the Vietnam War, allergic to rallying around the U.S. flag—was a huge emotional cultural change. The country was coming together to bring the American hostages home. By late March into spring, yellow ribbons flying from tree branches would remind us all of yet another day the Americans were being held against their will. Every piano player across Washington would get endless requests for a version of "Tie a Yellow Ribbon Round the Old Oak Tree."

But then the unthinkable happened.

The Hawks were circling.

Even from my piano I could hear them calling for the Dems' blood. Operation Eagle Claw not only had failed to rescue the hostages but had lost the lives of eight American military commandos in the Iranian desert. The operation took place on April 24, 1980. The objective was to rescue the 53 hostages, the majority being held at the American embassy compound, with others in the Foreign Ministry building and elsewhere. The mission brought together members of the four branches of service, including operators from Delta Force and elements of the 1st Battalion 75th Ranger Regiment, with personnel and units spread across the globe.

The U.S. Special Operations Command didn't exist yet. It wouldn't be activated by the Department of Defense until April 16, 1987. Instead, in Washington, under the direction of the president, the secretary of defense, the joint chiefs, and the national security advisor, a task force was put together to plan and conduct the mission.

The mission was extremely complex and left very little room for error. The first destination for the 132 Delta Force army Rangers, six air force C-130 Hercules fixed-wing planes (code-named Republics), and eight navy RH-53D Sea Stallion helicopters (code-named Blue-beards) was in the Dasht-e Kavir desert in Iran, termed Desert One.

In a relatively short amount of time, catastrophe would strike the rescue forces of Eagle Claw. After technical failures with three of the eight Bluebeards, those in command at Desert One decided to abort the operation when it was clear that only five choppers would be able to conduct the next part of the mission. The nightmare was just beginning.

There had been no rehearsal for a Desert One evacuation in case of an abort. Orchestrating the takeoff of a C-130 required Blue-beard 3 to move from its position. Because of the dust being generated from the propellers of his hovering chopper, the pilot could not see the position of the C-130 below. He could get a visual only on the airman on the ground directing him—who, in order to shield his eyes from the stinging sand, had moved underneath the wing of the C-130.

The blades of Bluebeard 3 ripped through the C-130 that was carrying heavy fuel reserves. Fuel and ammunition ignited, trapping many men in the back of the plane. Other men were jumping out of the only opening that was not blocked by fireballs and explosions. Many were injured. Eight were dead.

During his address to the nation Carter took full responsibility as commander in chief for the loss of life and mission failure. But that could not stop the emotional response from around the country.

Khomeini used the tragedy to validate his revolution, convincing many Iranians that this was a miracle, a righteous act of God against the Great Satan, America. Photographs of Khomeini and his supporters at the site of Desert One lacerated the heart of America, as the bodies of our dead soldiers were desecrated there in the desert.

With a collective reaction of *Enough!* from a large segment of the American population, dissonant chords were gaining momentum and echoing Nixon's reference to America as "a pitiful giant." In Washington, seeds of a battle cry called "the Revolution in Military Affairs" were being actively planted. Some would say Eagle Claw was the impetus to completely overhaul the Special Operations Forces. The result would be the establishment of the independent U.S. Special Operations Command, mandated by Congress in 1987. (They would be deployed in August 1990 under Operation Desert Shield after Iraq invaded Kuwait and was poised to invade Saudi Arabia and control the oil. We would then watch them on our screens in early 1991 during a televised war called Desert Storm.)

After the tragedy of Eagle Claw in April 1980, September ushered in what would become a protracted eight-year war between Iraq and Iran. "The enemy of my enemy is my friend" became a catchphrase, like a hook in a song.

ℓ ℓ ℓ

I often overheard Ronald Reagan's name being spoken as I made my way through the smoke to the piano. At one of the 1980 presidential debates, Reagan said, "A recession is when your neighbor loses his job. A depression is when you lose yours. And recovery is when Jimmy Carter loses his."

By November 4, 1980, the American hostages were still not home. All around the District, the yellow ribbons blew in the wind and I still played "Tie a Yellow Ribbon." When Reagan became the next president, the population of Washington was on the move yet again. And those people would visit me at the piano a few blocks from the White House. While I played a version of "The Tide Is High" from Blondie's *Autoamerican* LP, someone with cocktail in hand would recount how Carter's choice to give asylum to the shah had proven to be catastrophic for him. Across town, Tip O'Neill, the speaker of the House of Representatives, had publicly expressed outrage at the lack of support and funding for the Special Operations Forces.

And then there he was before me at the piano. It seemed like a lifetime ago that I was fourteen and playing for a congressional party. I had asked him what his job was and he told me he was the speaker. A little green at the time, I asked, "Speaker of what?" He laughed and I played some Irish songs while he danced a jig. He then requested "Bye Bye Blackbird" and we sang it together. He was a gentleman to me when I was not quite ready to deal with the complexities of Washington.

Then I was young and naïve. But at seventeen the gullible gloves were coming off, and it was obvious that the lessons I had been taught in high school, about how the government operated, did not tell the truth about the real power in Washington, which was in the hands of the lobbies and Big Corp.

Republicans may have won, but Reagan said, "I believe the very heart and soul of conservatism is libertarianism." The Libertarian

Party's vice-presidential candidate in 1980 was David Koch of the Koch brothers. Their platform in 1980 included abolishing the Environmental Protection Agency and the Medicare and Medicaid programs, repealing the minimum wage, not taxing Big Corp, and spending as much money as they wanted in order to own part of the Senate, the House, and possibly one day even the presidency.

Their message did not land with the average person. At the time, no one really bought into the idea that the superrich getting tax cuts would help the average working person, including those in the middle class. We knew that huge tax cuts for the superrich meant the road to serfdom for those who were not part of that club. It seemed the Libertarians' and Republicans' objective was, in essence, to create an economic aristocracy.

The gay maître d' would stand by my piano as I played "The rich get richer, the poor get laid off, ain't we got fun," and he would just shake his head and say, "Why would anyone willingly swallow the poison of that morally corrupt elixir? Do they really think we are that easily duped?"

After a roller-coaster ride of a year and a huge victory for Reagan and his supporters, an announcement was made that would shock the world.

The voice that taught us to "imagine all the people living life in peace" was silenced. John Lennon was murdered, shot in New York. The loss of a songwriter who had pushed us to think was unbearable. Candles were lit around the world. Songs he had brought to us were sung. We ended the year in collective mourning for a visionary soul that had been taken from us much too soon.

BANG

Bang went the gun on their tongue
word crucifixion toward immigrants shunned
"Immigrants that's who we all are
'cause we're all made of stars"
you said to them
oh yes you did
Bang went the Universe
Hydrogen lusting for Helium's burst
a mighty Sun's Dance of Death
Exploding Super Nova
one story's end
seeds another to begin

then the heavens
opened and then
I heard voices
joined in Hosannas
breathlessly I saw your star
so bright it blinded me
I had to shield my eyes
so bright it blinded me
I had to shield my eyes
so bright it blinded me

I had to shield my eyes
and then
you took my hand
oh yes you did

Bang the world now traumatized
by a cluster of hostile humans who side
with their warlords of hate
so we must out-create
with the Backbone of Night
to Rehumanize

then the heavens
opened and then
I heard voices
joined in Hosannas
and their tower
of confusion
could not drown
the Light
from your star
so bright it blinded me
I had to shield my eyes
so bright it blinded me
I had to shield my eyes
so bright it blinded me

resistance

I had to shield my eyes
and then
you lit the path
oh yes you did

"Can't you see"
he said to me
"that we all
are Molecular Machines"
goals and dreams
all I wanna be
is the very best
Machine I can be
Hydrogen
Calcium
Phosphorus
Potassium
Sulfur
Sodium
all I wanna be
is the very best
Machine I can be
Iodine
Iron
Manganese
Molybdenum

Nitrogen
Selenium
Silicon
Tin
Vanadium
and Zinc
all I wanna be
a MOLECULAR Machine

IMAGINE.

In an American court.

A little boy about four years old.

Of Latin descent.

Sandaled feet flouncing over the chair lip.

Huge ear defenders on.

A U.S. judge asks, "Do you have a lawyer?"

The little boy shakes his head.

"Do you know what a lawyer is?"

The little boy shakes his head again—after his headphones translate the words.

Zero-tolerance policy.

Parents separated from their children.

Children crying in cages.

Imagine.

The white power movement.

Those who are actively advocating for the destruction of people—whom they objectify as "other."

The architects behind zero tolerance . . .

What events did they twist to justify that policy?

The implementation of zero tolerance.

Being the reason that this little boy was sitting in that chair on his own, alone.

≀ ≀ ≀

In 2017 the Muses brought me to "Bang," which activated me to make a direct response.

At this specific moment in our travelogue, the vilification of Muslims was being dubbed a "travel ban." Through the writing of "Bang," I was reminded that we had to *out-create* the destructive solution being executed by the immigration architects in the Trump administration. The purpose of "Bang" was and is to encourage conversations on immigration and immigration reform. She refuses to be accused of being an advocate for "no borders whatsoever" or of being a borderless fantasist simply because she and I disagree with the extreme of no tolerance. Sensible people making sound, reasonable policy based on levelheaded facts—these people have to exist. "Bang" holds a space for those who are compelled, even if nervously, to explore the tough subject of immigration reform with a balance of pragmatism and imagination.

Some songs are not written to your ideological combatants. In this case, "Bang" was forged to energize and *align with* those who believe in a democratic process. Those who believe that supporting an authoritarian government—implicitly or explicitly—is completely against the concept of human rights.

There can be *Eureka!* moments in songwriting. You can be banging your head against an imagined wall, and then there's Carl Sagan talking to you through time. Through his science-mind, his explanation of what defines being human. Those thoughts were expansive. They were not confined to a religious dogma; all the same, they allowed people to hold on to that if they wanted to. And that's because Sagan did not "otherize" any of us in his definition of what a human is—not one of us. He did not undervalue or overvalue anyone because of religion or skin tone or gender.

He said, Humans are all made of star stuff.

Star stuff.

Imagine.

What is star stuff made of? That was my first reaction thinking about Sagan. *We humans are made of that very stuff?*

This transcended every definition of what I had learned a human was. Other definitions were simply a distraction from this key truth.

Through time, Sagan had shown me something beautiful in his definition. And this thought that he shared, talking from a computer screen, became precious to me and changed me. Maybe only incrementally, but change is change. The periodic table became part of my life for the first time. By taking on board a new thought, an idea that had not been a part of *how* I thought and who I thought I was . . . well, yes, this could be really scary. Change *can* be scary. Individually we live through our own tests and trials, through our own personal battles and losses. One day we are just taking for granted that we are achieving what we set out to do that day. We are in our routine—not that there can't be challenges, but we get through them. And then a hurricane, a fire, a mass shooting, a terrorist attack—an event forces us to cope with something we have not rehearsed for. *I have looked up and out, desperately talking to anyone, saying Help, please help—I am not prepared for what is in front of me.*

And sometimes I am met with no answer, a deafening response, no song at all. Not in that moment. We have all been forced to sit with ourselves—feeling not like we are made of star stuff but feeling overwhelmed. Where is the blueprint for this emotion?

Then there are devastating events that affect not just family and friends but a whole community, a city, something even greater. Some people use a tragic event to twist the narrative and push their own political agenda. These are the Warlords of Hate.

Others work through a tragedy by figuring out ways to process grief. And we all grieve differently: some of us shut down; some of us reach out. Some of us lash out. Some hours of the day convulse with torrents of shock. In other moments, we find ourselves left with a bleak numbness.

Collective trauma is its own energy.

Not only songs but whole albums have been written to document what people were telling me they were seeing and hearing and feeling. Written to document where someone was—within our collective story that was unfolding in real time.

At times I have been warned by the Muses, and the lessons from them can be tough and at times harsh. It's as if they say, "T, you need to respect where this person is in the grief process and that they are not at resolve. Even if it would make you more comfortable if they were, they are in their suffering. So if you are going to weave the truth of this moment into song, then you cannot project onto them. If you really want to document the emotion of this moment, then the key is to listen."

The most important skill a songwriter needs is to be able to listen. Like an elephant: ears the size of Kansas. Not only do you need to hear every beat of breath between what is being said; you have to hear what *isn't* being said.

With collective trauma, a group of people mourn together; each can truly have empathy for what the other is going through. Because their commonality is "this" particular tragedy, they are able to work through it—individually *and* together.

And there are times, when we are alone, that we may feel broken or divided into pieces inside, but then, because someone else, maybe someone we don't know or don't know very well, all of a sudden: *BANG.* They are mirroring a shattering familiar pain that you recognize, when you look in their eyes. *There* it is, right *there.* A shared feeling, a knowing . . . and you begin grieving together.

GIRL

from in the shadow she calls
and in the shadow
she finds a way
finds a way
and in the shadow she crawls
clutching her faded photograph
my image under her thumb
yes with a message for my heart
yes with a message for my heart

she's been everybody else's girl
maybe one day she'll be her own
everybody else's girl
maybe one day she'll be her own

and in the doorway they stay
and laugh as violins fill with water
screams from the bluebells can't
make them go away
well I'm not seventeen
but I've cuts on my knees
falling down as the winter
takes one more cherry tree

≀ ≀ ≀

she's been everybody else's girl
maybe one day she'll be her own
everybody else's girl
maybe one day she'll be her own

rushin' rivers
thread so thin
limitations
dreams with the flying pigs
turbid blue
and the drugstores too
safe in their coats
and in their dos
a smother in our hearts
a pillow to my dots
one day maybe one day
one day
she'll be her own

and in the mist there she rides
and castles are burning in my heart
and as I twist I hold tight
and I ride to work
every morning wondering why

₹ ₹ ₹

"Sit in the chair and be good now."
and become all that they told you
the White Coats enter her room
and I'm callin' my baby
callin' my baby
callin' my baby
callin'
everybody else's girl
maybe one day she'll be her own
everybody else's girl
maybe one day she'll be her own
everybody else's girl
maybe one day
she'll be
her
own

SONGS ARE LIVING, BREATHING things. "Girl" is not locked up in time or aligned only to the circumstances that propelled her birth in 1990. She can be applied not just to a young woman's story but to anyone at any age who has made a commitment to themselves. A commitment to stop being the person someone else needs, demands, or seduces them to be or intimidates them into becoming. Whether we become "this person" to deflect conflict or to stave off rejection, we have all morphed into "the me" someone else wants us to be.

Certain relationships can just wear you down. So you mirror or reflect back—kind of like a pet, reflecting back what its master wants. This can seem easier in the moment: *Whatever it takes to back this person's vibe down.* The master does not have to be male. Sometimes he is, but not always. Whoever the master is, they know this, that people can be trained. Either with praise, shame, the fear of failure, or the fear of being gaslighted, the technique is a relationship of rewards and punishments. There is no unconditional love here. No, this kind of relationship is all about the master's conditions. Not joint respectful mutual conditions, but *their* conditions.

The mantra of "Girl" is *I must become my own owner, my own authority. I must be a home to myself, and I must find a way to live what I believe.*

Finding out who you are as a person and what ingredients make up "you" is no easy task. Especially if you have been editing out *this bit* or *that byte* or even *megabytes* of yourself. You might feel like a faded picture of "the you" you wanted to be. The song "Girl" had me putting up dreamcatchers around the house to salvage pieces of myself that I myself had gaslighted.

Some aspects of myself were not being helpful anymore. So "Girl" would say, *That's natural. That part of you served her purpose. Thank her and let her go.*

"Just like that?" I'd ask.

Send her off with a margarita. She'll be fine.

Not only was she guiding me to embrace certain elements that I had diminished; she was encouraging me to be open to other sides I had not allowed myself to explore. I began to realize it was okay to tweak myself. Some of my tweaks were vast improvements.

But "Girl" was an important guide when she taught me, *Don't be afraid to grow and expand your sense of self as a person and as an artist. Who knows? You might like opera—one day. Maybe not today, but you will find yourself at different crossroads all through your life. Don't be afraid to create something different.*

"Girl" knew full well that in that moment in 1990, I was at yet another serious crossroads as an artist and battling powerful forces against potential song demolition. "Girl" had not yet been written, but she was listening from the ether to the massive music problem I faced all those years ago.

I know she was with me forming herself into a Song Being. I know this as I write to you on the thirtieth year of her birth in 2020.

In 1990 *Little Earthquakes*, my second album (and my first solo album), had just been rejected by my label, Atlantic Records. Some of you may know the story; some of you may not. I am not the first artist to have their record rejected, and I won't be the last. But the Muses have compelled me to share the complexities of the problem and how we found a solution that worked for me, the artist, and for the investor, the record label.

It goes without saying that there are many people involved when an artist and a project are in crisis and about to become audio road-kill. There are not enough pages to mention all the names, but I did not solve this shocking conflict all by myself. The following road map lays out the possible routes to take and to avoid in order to find resolve for all involved in a creative crisis.

There were several components to the problem. As I stated in my first book, the rejection of *Little Earthquakes* brought me to a standstill. It was not as if I hadn't faced rejection before; my first album, *Y Kant Tori Read*, had bombed in 1988. But I found the piano again—or I should say *she* found *me*—and the album *Little Earthquakes* was built around this rediscovery after my previous betrayal of the piano. From my point of view the songs and the artist and the recordings were speaking from a truthful place, and those who had worked on it felt that it had an old magic.

The rejection by the label and the solution that powerful men had come up with was traumatic, a slash-and-burn response: "Replace all the pianos with guitars."

The battle for the integrity of the songs and to protect those recordings was on, but how to fight? How to fight the opinion of someone at the label that had a lot of success as a producer and sold a lot of records, who came up with this solution: "Mute the pianos; insert the guitars. It should work."

Just so we are clear, I was freaking out. Melting down. Hyperventilating and throwing watermelons at walls. This decision was coming from the top at the record label, and there was no higher power.

I was signed to an eight-album deal, all of them the record label's option. That calculates to about sixteen years of your life if you are quite prolific and are recording one year and touring the next and the writing of the next album is happening on the road. That is, if you can keep up that writing-recording-touring marathon. More likely the artist is locked into a contract for about twenty years.

Also, the label owns the recordings you have made under contract with them. So if they do not want to sell you, it's their option, not yours. (I suggested they sell.) Alternatively they can shelve you, keeping you in a kind of Limbo, neither marketing your work nor selling your contract to another company; this can lengthen the process so that no one wants to buy you. This power labels have is very real. This was before the internet, so the labels were the only game in town and they knew that.

At the time of my rejection I was soon to be twenty-seven. And at that time in music history, pop culture had not yet reembraced the piano. With the folk music scene making a fresh mark with artists like Tracy Chapman and Suzanne Vega and many others, the acoustic guitar *was* proving itself, with critics and with sales. Synths were the keyboards of the day. The piano was seen as a snore and not fashionable, not from the point of view of the power brokers at the labels. (Elton and Billy were legends playing by different rules.) It is a different game that must be played when you are on the bottom of the music business food chain.

The only records I had sold from my first band's album, *Y Kant Tori Read*, were to my parents, Ed and Mary, and a few shocked Methodist parishioners and maybe a metal head in Idaho. Therefore I had yet to prove myself, to prove the piano was ready to carve a new place for herself in a snob-ridden pop culture playing for sinners—me being one—sweating out the demons with my left heel on the sustain pedal, singing for salvation, a sonic daughter of Jezebel with my right hip open to a southern church revival.

These were still only visions and only captured on the recordings that Atlantic owned and could contractually do with what they wanted. So my task was to negotiate that my songs of sin and redemption be kept pure. The Muses gave me a message: *You the songwriter might not be the most adept negotiator to come up with a solution that the men in power will agree to. The songwriter is only one component that makes up you the artist, and yes, she carries particular observational and emotional skills. But these men are not making a request. Their demand of "something different" must be served. In order to figure out what that is, it would be wise to assess what part of you and your training will best assist this challenging mission. Your complex task is to reject their solution to the problem but explain that you have heard their concerns, and then you must get them to agree to a different solution—which, by the way, you must come up with.*

To this day the Muses have me apply a technique I learned then, in 1990. They encouraged me to review my skills inventory, to find the part of me that has had some experience to apply to a current challenge.

The circumstances of that new challenge might not look like any circumstances from my past, but there might be something I can draw upon to pull into the frame. The one point the Muses were extremely direct about was that telling the record label "Go fuck yourself" was not an intelligent move. And would probably land me back in the piano bar circuit forever. I needed to break out of that trajectory to get the album back on track and out of gridlock. Guided by the Muses, I knew I needed to find my twenty-year-old, piano-bar-playing self. Together, sitting in my one-room apartment behind the Highland Methodist Church in Hollywood, we conjured the energy and perspective my piano-bar-playing self had learned by the spring of 1984.

The Muses asked, *At this time in your life, when you are being paid to play in Washington, can you fully be the artist you want to be?*

No, to be fair, for the most part I was there to serve the needs of the room.

Muses: *And in all these rooms, are the needs always different, or are there any similarities?*

Well, I guess the most obvious example of contrasting events would be when I would do a funeral and a wedding both in one day. Dad could pay me two-for-one on those days, so hiring me was a good deal—sort of like an early bird special. Not sure if he pocketed the rest, but it was a job and the energies were different. Weddings in many ways were less creative because the bride and groom naturally were quite specific about which songs were "their songs" and not a song they shared with an ex. So I followed the brief because if I played a love song I had not cleared beforehand, I could lose the room. Worse, I could cause hurt.

Muses: *And funerals?*

Funerals were usually heavy affairs with much less excitement unless there was tension over a will. Dad would usually know and would privately share if there were tensions or feuds going on. I probably would never see these people again unless they ran in the Georgetown or Capitol Hill set, where I played consistently. So he thought if explaining the situation would help me construct a calmer service through music, then he would have fulfilled his responsibility to the bereaved. There was usually more leeway in my choices during a funeral gig, though sometimes there were requests—a song or a hymn—but it was my job to set the tone and hold the space for that tone.

Muses: *Was the tone different in each of these rooms, including on Capitol Hill? Could the tone be compromised? And if so, how did you bring it back to that room's specific tonal center?*

Yes, the tone was specifically set for each room, and it was my job to understand what tone the client wanted. A funeral, a brunch after a graduation ceremony, a congressional cocktail party—there was a range within which I could lead a room, but there was always a tonal perimeter. My role was to read the room at all times and underscore the event. If someone got drunk and disruptive or an argument happened, there might be someone in tears by the piano. I'd play their request if I could, and that might bring more tears. Then I'd tell them I had a lot of requests and move into a rousing "New York New York," which would bring out the best and the worst singers to join in and lift the room's spirits.

Muses: *How many songs did you have by this point in your repertoire?*

Um, about a thousand or so songs that covered any style and

tone possibility that I could learn. I just never knew what in the collection would get a room out of a state of anxiety. Awkward moments might work on a theater stage, but they really are the kiss of death at a piano bar. I was known to move out of those as fast as I could, whatever it took.

It would always surprise me what would bring a room back to stability again. Southern gospel, puritanical Protestant, heavy metal, "Happy Birthday," swinging '60s, a rousing "God Bless America," '50s favorites, jazz standards, a Bach invention, country music, patriotic with a military flare—I've applied all of them to get a room out of awkward.

Muses: *Then you have in your skill set the ability to understand the structures of many songs with different tones?*

Yes, I guess I have studied the architecture of hundreds of songs, their arrangements and their Bones. You have to get to the Bones. The structural component of each song. Some would surprise me once I got in there with my "hearing light" on. All of this could help me to discern the tone DNA of each song.

Muses: *Let's thank your twenty-year-old self and invite her to come negotiate with the label alongside you, because now it is clear how you need to approach this.*

Is it?

Muses: *If they are suggesting you replace the pianos with guitars, that is only their solution to achieve a change of tone. Find a different solution. From what your younger self has said, in your Bones you know many different ways that tone can shift from song to song. You have chosen to go to battle in order to preserve the recordings. You have chosen to advocate for the piano. You have played for and been surrounded by men in positions of power wheeling and dealing in D.C. You have been able to serve the client's need for a specific tone. The men in power at the label are asking for a different tone. Offer them more songs with a different tone than the current one. An offering is what is needed. Add guitars to the piano or don't; that's just a detail.*

But I don't have any more to give.

Muses: *There is always more. We will send the energy. Expansion—that is the energy we will be sending you. You may need to make a pilgrimage to find the inspiration. Wherever you go we will find you. Just be open and put up no barriers.*

The Muses were right. I agreed to turn in four more songs, and this solution was received by the powerful men at the label.

Within a few weeks I was flying in to meet my parents in D.C., and then we drove to the old farm in the mountains of Virginia where my dad had grown up. At the farmhouse, memories came flooding back. My mom, Mary, and I would take long walks every day. My dad, Ed, spent most of his time on the tractor dealing with the garden. Mary would make supper with the vegetables from the garden and fruit cobbler from those trees that still ripened after all these years. There were no streetlights; the two-lane road was surrounded by hills and mountain land. There would be chats in rocking chairs. We would take walks up to a place called Roosterspur that used to be a creek way back when. Mom would talk to me about my journey up to that point—the ups and downs. She said, "You have made a commitment to the integrity of the music above all else. You know how to create in many different styles; there are limits only if you buy into the idea of creative limitation. But it has to come from devotion and not for commercial gain. When you create with the label's philosophy of a commercial model in mind, it has proven not to work. Whether that is a covenant you made to the Muses when you were a little girl, I am not sure.

"But if you create from the perspective of an artist in service I believe you will achieve what works for your standards and for their economics-driven philosophy."

One morning, walking through the old farmhouse, I passed the room where Grandma Amos would read her scriptures. We had disagreed on most things, even until she died when I was a teenager. She had elevated male authority, and I had made a commitment at a young age to fight that ideology as a feminist soldier for the Great Mother. Once she said to me, "One day, young lady, you will give your body and obedience to your husband and your soul to God." And I whipped around and said, "And what, pray tell, Grandma, are you saying is left for me?"

One evening during that visit in 1990, when Dad was in the other room watching the news and my mom was rocking in her rocking chair, I sat at the old upright piano. A melody began forming. She seemed to crawl through the veins of the earth and serpentine her way through the keys into my hands.

"Girl" stepped forward with a message for me.

I can help protect the other songs. If you are open to my potential, then together we can design my song to act as a bridge. A bridge that will take us from the style of the already recorded songs to the new Song Beings that are in process of forming.

"Girl" was able to bend and make herself the key bridge the record needed without betraying her artistic principles. She did not bend to any demands that she felt did not align with Her Mission. "Girl" taught me a lot and continues to teach me. She strives to become her authentic self every day and reminds me that I can expand how I see and hear my True North.

"Girl" can bend with the times.

During my Native Invader concert tour in 2017, "Girl" began to reframe herself. People coming to the shows were sharing that they were feeling traumatized by this large-scale and scary and political and divisive global rupture we were living through. The Muses began to show me that each concert would need to address this trauma. In every city in every venue. I had never seen this type of trauma. And I had been playing shows for forty years.

No, this was a ravenous beast of assault.

Not having been alive during World War II, I had no personal reference in my arsenal to this type of energy, on this scale. In every audience, every night, there was a combination of anxiety, grief, anger, and shell shock. But there was also a willingness on the audience's part to engage with all these emotions, together through songs, in order to shift the current energies. These energies were reacting to a brutal authoritarian bedevilment that was and is trying to hold the world hostage. Songs were called upon to help transform the malicious energies sown by this ravenous beast of assault.

"Girl" stepped forward. She understood that America was under attack.

"Girl" understood it was not only America that was under attack.

"Girl" worked with the other Songs, by forming a narrative, to combat the assault.

"Girl" was finding her relevance in the present day.

She told the story of being a girl that someone was trying to oppress, then she expanded her persona to a country, America, that authoritarians were trying to possess.

GIRL DISAPPEARING

7 am
so it begins again
1-0 (zip) favoring familiar silhouettes

left whips and chains
behind
I'm boycotting trends
it's my new look this season

riding on backs of palominos
Primed for an attack
it's as good
as good as it gets

with girl disappearing
what on Earth's occurring?
'cause she's right in front of me
a girl disappearing
to some secret prison
behind her eyes
she whispers
"Big Surprise. there was
no protection by this urban light.

so I'm running to
a constellation
where they can still see you"

Envy can spread
herself so thinly
She slipped in
before I could notice it

in my own war
blood in the cherry zone
when they pit
Woman against Feminist

riding on backs of palominos
ditching the blond shell
working her hell
on that red
carpet

with girl disappearing
what on Earth's occurring
'cause she's right in front of me
a girl disappearing
to some secret prison
but she's right in front of me
a girl disappearing

to some secret prison
behind her eyes
she whispers
"Big Surprise.
there was no protection
by this urban light.
so I'm running to
a constellation
where they can still see you"

then I'm running too
if that's a consolation
'cause I can still
see you

9/11/01. Midtown, NYC. 5:30 a.m.

The day started like any other day on the promo trail during a new record launch—a routine I had practiced for years.

1. Put kettle on.

2. Pull out choice tin of loose tea, a couple options available. (Usually black, but there are days for green.)

3. Get tea brewing in travel teapot. (Mesh preferred, as the cleanup is always more efficient.)

4. Hit the shower. Get all product out of hair, then off with the fake eyelashes, off with the liner, and off with the shadow from the day before. Normally, they would be slept in. (You never know when your hotel door buzzes and there's a fire drill or an evacuation. When you're a visitor of enough hotels, you never forget this.)

5. Alone in that shower you look back, you bring lessons from the past forward, even cringeworthy ones, and you anticipate what's coming. That's how you survive the promo dance. You accept, yet again, that there will be supporters and there will be those who want to take you down. This leads you to anticipating questions. So you deal with the facts. You retrace the development of the project at hand.

September 18 was the coming release day for *Strange Little Girls*. This was a record on which all the songs had been written by men— but were interpreted by me. Each song had a voice, a point of view from the song's anima. These voices had been developed over months with an extended think tank. The idea had begun in the Florida house as I rocked a three-month-old Tash in the rocking chair.

Parenting was a new adventure as we approached the first Christmas of the new century in the year 2000. Neil Gaiman, a fairy godfather to Tash, popped by to see how Mark and I were faring. Discussions soon orbited around concepts for the new album. It would be a covers record.

As a new mother I was drawn to the idea of a world where men are the mothers. Neil and Mark grabbed that idea with both hands: all the songs would have been mothered and born by men. These songs would then be retold from the point of view of a different woman that I would give voice to and embody for each song. Soon the think tank expanded to include others who offered songs written by men that spoke to them. The building of ideas then expanded to two of the people who would drive the visual team.

As always, Karen Binns was brought into the nucleus of the project early on. She and I have been collaborating as fellow artists since 1991 and continue to push each other creatively. Her expertise is translating a sonic story into its visual representation. Her offensive is an arsenal of film and fashion references to create a powerful still photograph. We joined forces with the legendary face transformer Kevyn Aucoin and worked for months on the visual representation of the characters. We bounced ideas off each other and the stories developed. They would have a sonic and visual representation of these women that we called "Strange Little Girls," based on a Stranglers song that was included on the album. Neil wrote a short story about each character for the album booklet after hearing and seeing the marriage of both think tanks.

Eight months after the seed for the new project had been planted in Florida, in December 2000, I played a launch gig at London's Union Chapel on August 30, 2001, during the middle of the European and U.K. promo. This was my first album launch with a baby involved. After the London gig, some of the crew went with me to do Canadian promo, while the rest would meet us in NYC. A few went with Mark and Tash to Florida. Mark and his team were prepping sound gear for rehearsals that would begin in two weeks for the Strange Little Tour, my first one-woman show in about seven years, since the tour for my second album, *Under the Pink*. We were bringing Tash, who had just turned one. Lists had been started: baby bumpers for her bus bunk, toys, the storybooks that, honestly, calmed the adults more than Tash. I thought, *Okay, it will be challenging, and the band will be missed on this one . . . but we got this. Just stay focused on the week's promo demands, on the project, and on being present.*

Eventually my part of the team made it to New York after our Canadian promo. That particular day we had to be out the door by 9:30 a.m., so hair and makeup arrived around 6:30. Preparations began for the U.S. promo week with Tony Lucia on hair and Lesley Chilkes, with whom I had worked extensively since 1991, on makeup. Room service was ordered. At 8:00 Karen Binns showed up with looks from London that she had begun designating for all the many different appearances.

We were matching up the next two weeks of events with Karen's London outfits when there was banging on the door, and Jerome Crooks, the tour manager, ran in, grabbed the remote, and turned on the TV.

It was about 8:45 a.m. when we stood and watched the North Tower being hit by the first plane. Of course, at the time we did not think about the plane being the "first plane." (Everyone who watched this moment will talk about where they were and will remember what they were thinking at that very moment.)

Jerome, Les, Tony, Karen, me—we all began voicing "what ifs" out loud. The thoughts started ricocheting off each other. Everyone was trying to make sense of such a horrific accident: *Maybe this happened. Maybe that . . . Traffic control . . . A pilot with a jammer . . .*

Your mind tries to weave that thread as fast as it can. The realization that you are not watching a disaster movie slams you into panic. And that there are real people on that plane—not extras on a huge set somewhere, but real people in that burning building, who had gotten up that morning and said, "See you after work," "See you for dinner," or "Will let you know when I land."

When the second plane hit, it was clear. It was not confusing. *Jesus Christ, we are under attack.*

In shock, some are able to give voice to what they are seeing—a primal sound of sheer terror. Others cannot feel their heart beating anymore, their blood chilled to the very depth of their bones.

A deafening silence, like one I have never experienced before or since, blanketed the room as the ghosts of crusaders past and present ravaged our skies. You never forget the horror on the faces of people watching, as victims of this massacre jumped or dove out of the tower's windows, away from hellfire explosions to their brutal deaths. The carnage would not stop as the minutes ticked on. And when we learned that there were more attacks, we would be hit in the frontal lobe of our brains, hearing in real time that two other planes, with innocent people on them, had been incinerated. That all the passengers had known their fate, that there were no angels or military might that could have saved them from the metal killing machines. From their grisly end.

A city under attack is not like an army under attack. Armies serve under a leader trained to command, and there is a rehearsed protocol; an ingrained discipline gets enacted. This city under attack was made up of small groups of people and lone individuals *stranded* within a mass exodus of millions. We had no blueprint for this. There was no instruction manual for this.

Instincts do kick in, but only once your blood has thawed and broken through your bone-wall of protection. A wall that your own inner beaver has built in lightning speed. Built to save you from being reduced to a puddle on a drab hotel rug.

Within a couple of hours, everyone in that hotel room began to act upon their reactions. They went to find their people. I went to the SIR rehearsal studios in Chelsea to find the crew. A rehearsal had been scheduled for later that day. But, of course, it was a given that everything that day would be canceled.

Yet crews stick together, so there we were, with our instruments and gear, wrestling with the shock. Cups of tea and mugs of coffee were made. The crew and the backline were there. My crew is always there for me. A huge iconic act that had scheduled the studio next to us had not arrived—in fact we were the only ones there—and I began to think, *Maybe we are nuts*. As in, really not all okay in the brain. And that might've been completely true. But this is what I knew: the discipline of rehearsal and the religion of *Find the piano, no matter what*. Or *Find the piano and the crew, no matter what*. Well, that can keep you almost sane.

Music was played. More often than not, it's the only thing I know how to do. Even if nothing is coming to mind, because my mind is all over the place, the piano finds my hands and guides them into song. There could have been nothing worth remembering in some of those meandering melodies channeled in that rehearsal room, or seeds could have been planted from those same melodies that would become part of *Scarlet's Walk*, an album not yet born.

I CAN'T SEE NEW YORK

From here
no lines are drawn
from here
no lands are owned
13,000 and holding
SWALLOWED
in the purring
of her Engines

tracking the Beakon
here
"is there a Signal
there
on the other side"

on the other side?
what do you mean
side of what things?

and you said
you did
and you said
you would find me
here

resistance

and you said you would
find me
even in Death
and you said
you said you'd find me

But I can't see New York
as I'm circling down
through white cloud
falling out
and
I know his lips are warm
but I can't seem
to find my way out
my way out I can't see
New York
as I'm circling down
through white cloud
falling out
and I know
his lips
are warm
but I can't seem
to find my way out
my way out
of this Hunting Ground

ι ι ι

From here
crystal meth
in meters of millions
in the end
all we have
soul blueprint.
did we get lost in it
do we conduct a search for this

"from the other side"
From The Other Side?
what do they mean . . .
side of what things?

and you said
you did
and you said
you would find me
here
and you said you would find me
even in Death
and you said
you'd find me
But I can't
see New York

resistance

as I'm circling
down through white cloud falling out
and I know
your lips are warm
but I can't seem to find my way out
my way out I can't see
New York
as I'm circling down
through white cloud falling out
and I know
your lips are warm
but I can't seem
to find my way
my way out
of your hunting ground
you again
it's you again
I can't see
I can't see
New York
from the other side

from the other side.

The Rev. Dr. Edison McKinley Amos, 1983

May the Joy of that First Christmas fill your home with Happiness

Epworth Chapel Parsonage Family: Edison, Mary Ellen, Mike, Marie & Ellen Amos

ABOVE: *Ed and Mary, 1949*

LEFT: *Family Christmas Card, 1970*

ABOVE: *Mary Ellen Copeland (Mom), 1947*

LEFT: *Poppa with Mary Ellen Copeland, 1930s*

At 17, Student Sings a Song of Success

By KATHRYN TOLBERT

Washington Post Staff Writer

BY JAMES A. PARCELL—THE WASHINGTON POST

Ellen Amos singing and playing at the Capital Hilton Bar.

Scene one: The Capital Hilton bar. Dim lights, ice clinking in glasses, laughter a little too loud. To one side of the room, at the piano, a woman leans into the microphone and sings, "Some say love, it isn't easy..."

Scene two: The living room of a two-story brick house on a winding suburban street. The same young woman, a high school senior, is perched at one end of the sofa. "I want to be a legend," she says unabashedly.

Another star-struck teen-ager with an ear for music and dreams of the pop charts? Perhaps. Or then again, Ellen Amos may one day be the hit recording artist that she is determined to be.

And if legends are born in places like Eastern Junior High School in Silver Spring or Richard Montgomery High School in Rockville, she is well on her way.

There they know Ellen for her renditions of the pop hits as well as for her own songs and for her love of singing and playing for an audience.

"I was a star at Eastern, but I tell you, that doesn't get you on the radio," she says realistically.

Her senior class elected her homecoming queen, but already her sights are set beyond high school, which she calls a "hobby that sometimes gets in the way."

"One of the reasons I'm an entertainer is because my father's a minister," she explained. "I meet so many people and get so much attention."

The Rev. Dr. Edison Amos of the Rockville United Methodist Church wholeheartedly supports his daughter's ambitions. For a year, he and his wife Mary Ellen spent every Friday night in the restaurant-bar called Mr. Smith's in Georgetown while Ellen, then 14, sang.

"Most of us who grew up during the World War II years want our kids to go to college," said Rev. Amos. "But I've found in counseling parents that some parents have a psychological mindset that works to the detriment and sometimes the devastation of youngsters. I've come

to realize that for her, we have to change for her if she's going to become a national recording artist."

"My concern is to get her into entertainment without her entering a lifestyle that is self-destructive," he said.

Amos, who has played the piano since the age of 3 and read music before she could read words, cut her first single this fall, "Walking with You" on one side and "Baltimore" on the other. She wrote "Baltimore" in honor of the Baltimore Orioles, hoping they would win the American League's eastern division title. Baltimore mayor William D. Schaefer gave her a citation of merit last month for the song.

She took music lessons at the Peabody Institute of Music in Baltimore when she was in elementary school, and has been studying voice and music at Montgomery College for the past five years.

Sometimes she feels obligated to justify her love for popular music: "What's good singing? You're just

appealing to people's likes and dislikes. Who's to criticize? What they like sometimes is what they hear the most."

Songs by the Beatles, James Taylor and Julie Andrews are high in her repertoire that includes most of the popular tunes since the 1940s. Since singing at Mr. Smith's, Ellen has performed at dozens of parties, clubs, schools, colleges and even basketball games. In November, the Capital Hilton signed her for a month, and she'll be back there next year.

For a 17-year-old raised in a minister's well-disciplined home, where is the common ground with the lifestyle and experiences that rock stars sing about?

"I think I'm perceptive. You don't always have to go through things to feel them," she said. "Being a minister's daughter, I could tell the moods of people my father counseled. I've been through a lot because so many people I know have been through a lot."

Ellen Amos: The Marbury Woman

BY ROGER PIANTADOSI

There was music coming out of this newish-looking brick building on M Street the other night — a sultry female voice, singing something by Stevie Nicks. Coming right out of the building, it seemed. My companion and I exchanged unknowing looks. We remained cool, however, because this was Georgetown, and we were already on thin ice.

Underdressed, that is: no feathers, no leather, no wet look. Just jeans with only one zipper apiece, and shirts with buttons. Cautiously, we investigated.

NIGHTLIFE

Glad we did.

The musical building, at the corner of 30th and M, is the Marbury House — a rather low-visibility, 164-room hotel under recent new ownership. Since they appeared about three years ago, the Marbury's brick arches and covered driveway haven't said a whole lot to passersby. Nowadays, however, they say more. Or sing, actually.

The music comes through speakers, from the Marbury's Lion's Gate Taverne inside — a relatively tiny, undistinguished hotel bar made substantially more distinguished by the source of that voice: one Ellen Amos. Age: 20. Appearance: 10 (as in the movie). Energy level: 7.5 (as in Richter).

Amos, who is also occasionally known as Tori, may very well be a famous pop star someday. An accomplished pianist and gutsy singer, this Rockville minister's daughter entered the Peabody Conservatory at age five but dropped out at 11 because, among other things, she was prone to apply a Beatles sensibility to Beethoven sonatas.

The other night, she demonstrated this happy sacrilege by whipping Beethoven's Sonata in F Minor into something even a fat man in a blue business suit could dance to. (The man in the suit, however, preferred merely to turn around in his seat and wink. This happens a lot — but less often after 10 p.m., when more people come specifically to listen to Amos, and fewer wear suits.)

Amos has been on the lounge circuit around Washington since she was (no lie) 13; now that she no longer has to arrive at work with a legal guardian, she's been to the West Coast twice this year for some exploratory studio work. For the time being, however, she can be found — free of admission, and free of pretension — every Monday through Friday night, 6 till about 11:30, at the baby grand amid the 50 soft seats of the Lion's Gate.

Ellen Amos: making the rafters ring and bricks sing.

Singing her heart out, mostly, and possibly yours.

My companion leaned over to whisper to me as Amos sipped hot tea from a wine glass after playing two requests — "Tiny Dancer" and (I didn't believe it either) "The Marine Corps Hymn" — plus a funky original (of which she has no end). Amos did all three with much feeling and finesse.

"Don't tell anyone about this place," said my friend.

Sure.

LION'S GATE TAVERNE — At the Marbury House Hotel, 3000 M Street NW. Open 4 p.m. to about 1 a.m. daily. No food (available downstairs in Tom & Jimmy's Restaurant until 10:30 p.m.); drink prices are reasonable for a hotel — especially one in Georgetown. No live entertainment Saturday or Sunday, but hotel manager Louis Marcus says it's planned, and probably live jazz. Tables outside — under the speakers — in nice weather. Brunch on Sundays (this Sunday with Amos at the piano). 726-5000.

Marbury Woman, 1984

LEFT: *Mary and Tori, 1984*

BELOW: *Piano Bar at The Marbury House, 1983*

Successful pop-rock pianist/composer Tori Ellen Amos attended the Peabody Prep from the age of five, studying piano and music theory. By the age of thirteen, she was playing piano for tips in Washington, D.C. clubs, and now she performs her own music in clubs all over the country. "I've been trained by the best, and I have to respect that training," Ellen says about her Peabody days. "The problem was—you see, I had this ear. I could hear anything and play it back to you verbatim. And I would improvise on things, and they don't like that. They said, 'No, no! You have to read.'"

ABOVE: Peabody News, *1985*

RIGHT: *Sister Marie, 1979/80*

AFTER A WHILE, a few of us left the rehearsal studio and began to walk toward Downtown. There were a lot of people walking every which way. The subways had shut down. All airplanes were grounded except for those used by the military or law enforcement. We walked a long way, until the burning of metal found a home in our throats. I couldn't stop coughing, so we turned back.

Letterman had gone dark, and no one was sure when it would be back on the air. I had done the show many times before and was set to do it that week with the album release. Jerome learned that there were tour buses fleeing the city. You could get out, but it was not easy to get back in. There was a rock bus headed to Miami with people who had kindly offered me a bunk if I wanted a lift. But it just didn't feel right to leave the city at that time. I had spoken with Mark for a few minutes right after the second plane hit. But after that I could not get a call out to anybody.

Some of the crew came back to my hotel to eat something. A buffet was prepared in the main dining room. An older lady was taking food from the buffet and putting it in her handbag. Fear was in her eyes—not knowing if there would be food in the morning.

On that very day George W. Bush would say, "Immediately following the first attack, I implemented our government's emergency response plans. Our military is powerful, and it's prepared. . . . We will make no distinction between the terrorists who committed these acts to those who harbor them. . . . America and our friends and allies join with all those who want peace and security in the world, and we stand together to win the war against terrorism. . . . America has stood down enemies before, and we will do so again."

The drums of war had begun beating.

One of the crew from Europe voiced what came to be proven true very soon: "That's it—there it is. The Hawks are in total and complete control. War has been declared. Declared on anywhere they decide is harboring a terrorist."

The elderly lady stuffing food in her bag had the fear of World War III in her eyes. And as I write these words all these years later, we are still at war—in that very same war.

On the streets of New York in the days following 9/11, survivors tacked up white sheets of paper pleading for news of the missing, a photo of their coworker or loved one looking out at you. In that moment, you found yourself holding a brief private vigil for this person you hadn't known but now wanted to know. And then you would be in front of another piece of paper with a different stranger's face, immortalized in that frozen frame but lost somewhere in the present.

And all the while planes would be circling overhead.

Soon I would begin to put these overwhelming emotions into songs, emotions that I could not explain any other way. To this day it is impossible for me to find the words to paint the tone that I was hearing at that time. And that is because there was not just one tone. And not just one song to encapsulate what was happening.

By the end of that week, *Letterman* was still dark and there was no telling when that would change. We had a scheduled "in-store" to sign albums at Union Square set for September 19, but until then everything, meaning all promo, was naturally—or unnaturally— on hold. Jerome had found an empty tour bus that was waiting in New Jersey, and I wanted to see Tash and Mark. In the music industry, road crews travel by bus, except for maybe Iron Maiden, who mostly fly themselves on their tours. But most crews hug the road hard—and I usually follow the crew's move. So, along with a pair of drivers, Lesley (makeup on the promo team), Tony (hair), Jerome (tour manager), and I set our course for Florida.

We would stop only for gas and food. *Just get to Florida* was our mind-set. Because we never knew when we would have to turn back.

Once we passed the Mason-Dixon Line, getting farther south, the stares were real. I can still see them burned into my mind's eye. And what they wanted to say had to be *NOT ONE of you is from around here*. We were a group made up of Les from the fashion world, her lips matte-red at all times; Tony of New York and New Jersey, a proudly gay Latino; Jerome, a cool business brain from L.A., African American; a feminist, scruffy-looking me; and those two tour bus drivers, who would clock a few thousand miles in a very few days.

As we sat down as a group to eat, the waitress simply asked, "So where are y'all from?"

As soon as we said, "We've just driven from New York City," the hugs began. Truckers and waitresses would come over. There was no North-South divide. There was no divide at all.

There was an exchange of true compassion.

This happened too in the deep, deep South, where Les's British accent was not understood and I needed to partially translate our waitress's long-tall-glass-of-sweet-tea southern drawl to our little gang. And even here there was no divide, no discrimination toward any of us.

This despite the fact that we were traveling after evangelist Jerry Falwell had been a guest on Pat Robertson's *700 Club*. At one point during the program, Falwell had begun blaming who he believed was behind the 9/11 terrorist attacks, reasoning, "What we saw on Tuesday, as terrible as it is, could be minuscule if, in fact, God continues to lift the curtain and allow the enemies of America to give us probably what we deserve." He then said, "The abortionists have got to bear some burden for this because God will not be mocked. And when we destroy 40 million little innocent babies, we make God mad. I really believe that the pagans, and the other abortionists, and the feminists, and the gays and the lesbians who are actively trying to make that an alternative lifestyle, the A.C.L.U., People for the American Way, all of them who have tried to secularize America, I point the finger in their face and say, 'You helped this happen.' "

Robertson responded, "Well, I totally concur, and the problem is we have adopted that agenda at the highest levels of our government."

These were people who were not being helpful with their words. One could call their kind of blame blind morality. And there were people claiming that they saw Muslims cheering in New Jersey when the Towers went down. There were people making a conscious choice to be opportunistic with this horrible tragedy. To rile the public to an all-consuming anger. Yes, the terrorist attack was evil. But grooming a country while it was in mourning to invoke a specific God and to pray from a place of hate was also evil.

This was the day before the prayer service at the National Cathedral in Washington, which took place on September 14. At the prayer service President Bush told the crowd, "Our responsibility to history is already clear: to answer these attacks and rid the world of evil."

PANCAKE

I'm not sure who's fooling who here
as I'm watching your decay
we both know you could deflate
a 7 hurricane
seems like you and your tribe decided
you'd rewrite the law
segregate the mind from body from soul

You give me yours
I'll give you mine
'cause I can look your God right in the eye

You give me yours
I'll give you mine
You used to look my God
right in the eye

I believe in defending
in what we once stood for
seems in vogue to be a closet
misogynist homophobe

a change of course
in our direction
a dash of truth

spread thinly
like a flag on a popstar
on a benzodiazepine

You give me yours
I'll give you mine
'cause I can look your God right in the eye

You give me yours
I'll give you mine
You used to look my God
right in the eye

Oh Zion please remove your glove
and dispel every trace
of his spoken word
that has lodged
in my vortex

I'm not sure who's fooling who here
as I'm watching our decay
we both know
you could deflate a 7 hurricane
you could have spared her
oh but NO
messiahs need people dying in their name
you could have spared her

resistance

oh but no
messiahs need people dying
in their name
you say, "I ordered you
a pancake"
you say, "I ordered you a pancake."

THE REALIZATION: I WAS on the road bearing witness. Witnessing how one cataclysmic event can have opposite reactions in people. Reactions that will still be affecting not just America but the whole world eighteen years later. Ground Zero will be used to justify Zero Tolerance by the architects of that brutal policy. Ground Zero will be weaponized to enter a seemingly never-ending war.

Just a few hours after we made it to Florida, the phone call came. We needed to get back on the bus and return to NYC. The first *Letterman* show after the tragedy would be without music, but I would play a song on his second show.

I had been encouraged to cancel the tour because other artists had decided to cancel. Some bands were stranded in the cities where they had been scheduled to play because so many venues had gone dark and would stay dark for over a week. But before I got back on the tour bus I stood outside and looked at the Indian River and tried to figure out the right thing to do. Just because other artists were making decisions that were right for them, as they considered their specific set of circumstances, did not mean that what they decided was right for me.

Mark told me, "Look, Wife, I'm there whatever you want to do."

And I said, "You know what, Husband, if I felt in my bones that we were going to put the people who come to the shows in danger, then I'd make the phone call and say we're pulling out. But as you are standing there holding Tash, I know the three of us, along with our crew, need to be out there bearing witness to what's really going to happen next. We need to exchange information with people who will have different perspectives and access to different information, and only then will we really get a sense of what is happening across the country. And in my bones, it feels right to tour."

The bus ride back to New York was quiet. We were all in our own thoughts. The idea that America was in a position of strength did not leave me. A position of strength like one I had not seen in my lifetime. There was an outpouring of love from so many people around the world. We didn't have to act rashly. We could be prudent.

Imagine: the most powerful nation in the history of the world not lashing out and rushing to the unimaginative macho response: violence.

As the bus took us out of Florida and back into the Deep South, I found myself trying to will those in Washington to find their wisest selves and not their paranoid selves. *Surely all the policymakers will think this through. Really really really think this through . . . The unbelievable responsibility, to have the most powerful military in the world and not just unleash death.*

The discipline it takes *not* to react impulsively and just bomb the hell out of the bastards is true discipline implemented by wise men and women, especially when you have the troops and the artillery to flatten any city. The discipline it takes to gather information and *not* to make the obvious move that most men in power make—that is, to show strength through violence.

The wheels on the bus kept turning.

Imagine: America could carve out a path for herself and, yes, find and capture the terrorists who were behind this, but by being strategic and wise. With cunning and relationship building, a new world could be forged. Now that is what power in the right hands looks like. A chief that everyone in the tribe looks to in times of crisis because he walks through and plays out in his mind every move he could make. He knows what his enemies want him to do. He has people around him to challenge his strategies, seeing potential outcomes, how certain moves could play into his enemies' hands. This is Prudence. Dear, undervalued Prudence. Imagine this kind of leader in times of crisis. A leader who serves America first. Not business interests. Not rich cronies and defense contractors who will get richer on the bloody backs of our boys and girls.

No, we need a commander in chief who loves America more than they love their business deals or their predilection for vengeance against those who question their motives. This is the prudent question that a responsible war council would ask: What is driving you to do what you are about to do, Mr. President? And then that council has to hold that president accountable to what the office commands or they should resign out of their dedication to our country.

As the bus headed north, I felt hope. America could be that example of the "right use of power" so that disenfranchised young men wouldn't find it appealing to join the killing squads. And that could happen because America would have shown that we are rational and not how we had been portrayed by Islamic extremists.

By now we were in the Carolinas.

What song should I play on Letterman*?*

It had been almost a week since the attack on America. At truck stops and off-road cafés, some people expressed frustration and bewilderment. People were wounded. Feelings were raw. There was a huge emotional gash exposed in everyone we saw. But how that gash was going to heal had not been decided yet. What if that wound did not fester and become infected but actually healed? Yet in order to heal there had to be knowledge. And to get knowledge, tough questions had to be asked. And those answers might have made us take stock of what our leaders had been up to. Maybe we had to approach the world in a different way. Strategically and with stealth. And although the word "war" had been spoken by the president, the people's narrative was not committed to that yet. Being on the road for a few thousand miles in only a few days helped me to bear witness to this fact.

And no, I hadn't been on the West Coast. The West Coast, specifically Santa Monica, where one of the future architects of Zero Tolerance was in high school. His name was Stephen Miller, though I didn't know that then. And over the weeks and years and years and years and to this day, it is clear that some people have chosen to politicize the horror that was 9/11 to activate their policies. It is also clear that two divergent viewpoints and two Americas would forge their own divergent paths in the long term and that the 9/11 narrative would be hijacked by the Hawks in a few days' time.

But I was there. And I did not encounter hate in New York City or over thousands of miles being on the road documenting what I saw. I discovered grief and pain and loss. And I saw people from different cultures sharing cigarettes together, listening and communicating, and holding each other in an understanding. It was beautiful to see.

The responsibility of being the first music on *Letterman* weighed on me heavily. I considered "Imagine," but that song did not answer the pain I had seen up and down the East Coast. The song I chose would have to look directly at the nation's pain and reflect that pain back. So I decided to play a song called "Time", by the great songwriter Tom Waits, which I had sung on the *Strange Little Girls* album.

The night after I played *Letterman*, I did an album signing at the Virgin Megastore in Union Square. The lampposts were still papered with the faces of those still lost. Vigils were still taking place, candle flames blowing in the wind but not blowing out.

A lot of people came to visit me that night. To tell me all kinds of things. One young man said, "I am not a fan of your music, but I have lost my uncle and I had no place to go." We held each other in an embrace; the tears were real from both of us. Others warned that we were on the verge of war—that the Hawks were *set* on a big war. And others said, "No matter what happens, do not capitulate to pressure, from God knows where, to cancel the tour."

The reason one person gave me was frank but ominous: "We need a place to gather to exchange information that we know is secure. In a way, the task of the tour is to help us do that. The fact that there is music involved is just a backdrop for some of us. I hope that does not offend you."

Okay, I thought. *I can hold that space.*

The next day, September 20, 2001, the president addressed Congress and the nation. At a certain point he said, "Now this war will not be like the war against Iraq a decade ago, with a decisive liberation of territory and a swift conclusion. It will not look like the air war above Kosovo two years ago, where no ground troops were used and not a single American was lost in combat.

"Our response involves far more than an instant retaliation and isolated strikes. Americans should not expect one battle, but a lengthy campaign unlike any other we have ever seen. It may include dramatic strikes on TV and covert operations secret even in their success.

"We will starve terrorists of funding, turn them one against another, drive them from place to place until there is no refuge or no rest.

"And we will pursue nations that provide aid or safe haven to terrorism. Every nation in every region now has a decision to make: Either you are with us or you are with the terrorists."

Someone at a radio station showed me a list of banned records, that is, songs that could not be played on air in light of the tragedy. It didn't surprise me that songs with the words "airplane," "fire," and "crash" in the title were on the list. But then I saw one word.

Imagine.

"Imagine" had been banned.

The radio guy said to me, "Can you believe those clowns banned 'Imagine'?"

My response to him was, "Yes, I can actually believe that the Hawks would want to ban 'Imagine.' They banned it because songs can be dangerous. And the ideology of 'Imagine' is everything that they do not want the masses to remember."

And the Strange Little Tour began on September 28, 2001.

FATHER'S SON

steady girl on your feet
you and your wonderings
bread can feed a few
so can some cartoons

so it ends so it begins
I'm my Father's Son
plant another seed of hate
in a trusting virgin gun

steady girl for the show
God versus God ringside
littered with corpses
neither God can forgive
so the desert blooms
strawberry cactus
can you blame Nature
if she's had enough of us

so it ends
so it begins
I'm my Father's Son
plant another seed of hate
in a trusting virgin gun

꜀ ꜀ ꜀

steady boy watch them pray
to You I suspect
if you keep my flesh firm
I'll ready those sacraments

so it ends
so it begins
I'm my Father's Son
so it ends
so it begins
I'm my Father's Son
plant another seed of hate
in
another
Father's
Son

AT 9:59 P.M. ON SEPTEMBER 27, 2018, RAINN—the Rape, Abuse and Incest National Network—sent a message across its platforms: "We are experiencing unprecedented wait times for our online chat. If you are able, we encourage you to call 800.656.HOPE (4673) or reach out via chat tomorrow. If you are in immediate danger, call 911."

In excruciating detail, Dr. Christine Blasey Ford had told the Senate Judiciary Committee about being sexually assaulted by the U.S. Supreme Court nominee Brett Kavanaugh when she was fifteen. When she was asked during the hearing how she could be sure it was Kavanaugh that had attacked her, she said, "Norepinephrine and epinephrine encode memories into the hippocampus. . . . Indelible in the hippocampus is the laughter." According to her testimony, she remembered the laughter of her assailants, of the two young men who had been in that room with her. She was 100 percent positive it was he.

Between the Thursday and the following Sunday after her testimony, RAINN experienced a 338 percent increase in hotline traffic. In fact, since RAINN had been established in 1994, Friday, September 28, the day after Dr. Ford's testimony, was the busiest day in the hotline's history.

This was a pivotal moment. Pivotal because whatever emotions that excruciating hearing brought up in the country, the number of calls to the hotline was evidence that sexual assault survivors refused to *disappear*.

People as well as organizations such as RAINN called on the Senate to delay the confirmation vote and reopen Kavanaugh's background check to investigate the allegations. Instead the Senate gave the FBI one week to report its findings. According to former FBI officers, however, a proper examination could not be conducted in the short time allotted. Therefore, because of those who hold the power in the Senate, there was no criminal investigation.

The ramifications of all that surrounded this hearing are ongoing. Protecting Kavanaugh from an FBI investigation has had, I believe, a domino effect. But not, perhaps, the domino effect some GOP senators had planned. The problem they and their enablers did not count on was that the dominos have not only knocked down other dominos, sliding Kavanaugh into his very own Supreme Court leather, Gilded Age chair; the dominos have created a tsunami in the other direction, knocking down any vestige of faith we had held on to that our senators cared about women survivors of sexual harassment and assault in America.

As Senator Mitch McConnell said, "We're gonna plow this through." And Mitch, you did. Well done. You achieved that. You plowed through with a ruthlessness similar to what women have experienced for thousands of years.

The message from these men is very clear:

We say what we want.

We do what we want.

We take what we want.

And we have the back of any other male who thinks like us.

Hall passes are available for White Male Privilege and for the women complicit with their behavior, women who are willing to look the other way.

In just one day we experienced two completely different testimonies, each person saying they were 100 percent sure theirs was the truth. As the television cameras captured and broadcast this modern tragedy, we as a country found ourselves at a crossroads. And what a crossroads it was, with all the implications of moral corruption from the people who held the power and the people who were the money behind them.

What happens when someone commits perjury? Isn't that a crime? Or does this not apply to judges and attorneys general? We the People, as a collective, didn't have closure on this—and we might never have closure on this.

Because these circumstances called for a criminal investigation. People have come forward stating that they believe Kavanaugh lied about the meaning of this phrase or that phrase—under oath. We do know that some very powerful men handed him one of the most powerful seats in the world. Everyone could see that what was implicit here was a quid pro quo.

I'll never forget a record mogul saying to me when I was in my twenties, "Tori, what are you doing? Are you out of your mind? Tori, what are you doing? You, young lady, are never going to get anywhere in *this* business unless you understand three words. Tori, three little words: *quid pro quo*."

You can imagine my face: "What are *you* talking about?"

But honestly, it was some of the best advice I have ever been given. I'm paraphrasing what he said over thirty years ago, but this was my takeaway from that lesson: "Nothing is for free. Nothing in this business. Everything is a trade-off. You help me, I help you. Now these things are not always straightforward, Tori, so beware what someone expects in return. Sometimes it's financial, which is basically straightforward, although you better get yourself a good attorney who can get his or her calls through to business affairs. But sometimes it's other stuff. And it's the other stuff, Tori, you need to have your eyes wide open about.

"It can be anything. Down the line even, when they call it in. 'It' is what you need to be clear about up front. But mark my words, 'It' will be expected; everybody has to pay back being helped out.

"No no. Not just helped out. What are we really talking about here—not just helped, Tori, okay? No. We're talking, we're talking *hauled* out of a situation—hauled out of some very hot water.

"This is very simple but very important, young lady. Very important. The bigger the 'help' given, the bigger the expectation of return. There must be a return, Tori, on the investment. There must be. That's fair. That's very fair. That's how it works, right? You got it? Good."

Plow this through was no minor message.

For someone to go from potentially being completely ruined to being catapulted to the highest court in the land—as the record mogul would say, "Tori, forget about it, that is no little quid pro quo."

The smug senators don't think we have any idea what happened

with Kavanaugh. Politically I probably don't. Who knows who owes what to whom? Who knows who puts money into what person's super PAC? Some of that will have to play out, and then the clever people who hunt down the facts will connect the dots and one day we will learn more.

But I do know something about modulation. A modulation does not have to be loud to create a tremendous impact, a tectonic shif Ever since Dr. Ford's testimony, women have told me they can't back to approaching issues as they had before. They will not co tinue trusting that politicians will work out important issues in a and considered manner.

Many women have told me that they are carving out time in week to become *engaged*. To commit to understanding the issu speak to them. They have been "called." This is their *Call to* Some are nurses, teachers, in the tech industry; some are s The conversations I have had with women from all over th try have solidified my faith in what women can achieve— when we exchange ideas. When we share our experiences other. Everyone has their own story and their own persp cannot be replaced by someone else. I am stating it plain Call to Action. Now is the time.

It's been over a year since Justice Kavanaugh was seat.

The effect of *Plow this through* has put all artist position. Some have to wait to intersect with the m moment to create that meaningful work. If you fee called, give yourself permission and acknowledge

moment for you. *Plow this through* is a battle cry to rally those who will fight to subdue women and attack our right to make choices for ourselves.

The message: The patriarchy and the women who serve them *will make your choices for you.* Choices for your body and for your life that you must live with forever. "Forced labor"—even in cases of rape or incest by a predator—is the planned harvest of *Plow this through.* And if you refuse to submit to this real-life *Handmaid's Tale*, then you can be jailed for the rest of your life. *Plow this through.* Their simple but sharp hook tells us everything we need to know.

The response from the Muses for artists, whatever the form your art takes, is to scatter fertile creative seeds into our Great Mother, giving her thanks for all she does for her daughters and sons. Male artists are being called to join their sisters in planting seeds to confront the corruption of those who would subject Earth's Daughters to the Patriarchal will. The question must be asked: Why do these men want to impregnate American women, even through a violent act?

"Ophelia" is a song that has stepped forward to be part of a very divisive and painful discussion. "Ophelia" chronicles the vast emotions a survivor will face.

The song is a warning. A warning to be vigilant in a culture of predator worship but also to see through those who make excuses for a predator's behavior and who help them continue abusing.

OPHELIA

Ophelia your secret is safe
Ophelia you must break the chain
some girls will get their way
some fathers will control from the grave
Ophelia you must remember
Veronica's America is not like—
is not like Charlotte's, one to savor
cosmic flavor
then Alison whispers, "remember
Change waltzes in with her sister Pain
waiting for you to send her away
wish her well break the chain
break the chain"
Ophelia
"The Eve of St. Agnes"
a poem
he can't reach you in
Ophelia you know how to lose
But when will you learn to choose
those men who choose to stay
those mothers who won't look
the other way
Ophelia you must remember
Veronica's America

is not like Charlotte's
one to savor cosmic flavor
Then Alison whispers,
"remember Change waltzes in
with her sister Pain
waiting for you to send her away
wish her well break the chain
Break the Chain"
I feel you
Ophelia

A DRUM AND BASS groove greeted me and Karen Binns as we walked down the street in 1993, a book under my arm. She and I were in a deep discussion about how women could be abusive to each other and the many different ways that can play out. I didn't know it, but in that very moment a song was being born. A song that has sparked varied interpretations by its listeners in the past twenty-seven years.

Once a song leaves my lair, it will form relationships that I have no control over and really should not want to have control over. But the fact is each song does have a genesis. Do I consciously know every aspect of the pollination process that creates a song? No. Sometimes it is a listener who points out what they have learned about a song. They may have had an experience that aligns with a song's inner secrets, secrets that may be hiding in the shadows that will take me years to discover or will take a listener years to share their interpretation with me.

As I have said for over thirty years now, I am only a cocreator of the songs. This is a working collaboration that has been witnessed in action by a few of those I have made records with. The Muses and the songs themselves offer melodies, chords, words, and tones that allude to what the sound must be. Just because I don't fully under-stand a tone does not mean I throw it away and impose my own. A tone may lead me to a discovery of a word or a phrase that reflects the tone originally sent by the Muses.

This is why I refer to songwriters as sonic hunters. Tracking down what a song wants to be requires being open to converging narratives.

"Cornflake Girl" is the song that was forming herself as I walked down that street with Karen all those years ago.

Karen had allowed me into her language world in 1991. We had been speaking in this language for a couple of years. Our way of communicating consisted of renaming a word with its reference. For example, we would refer to serial saboteurs as Cornflake Girls.

Another important element of our conversation about why and how women betray each other was the groove underscoring our chat. The swing feel blaring out of a shop that day is known as a shuffle groove. I found it really difficult not to sway back and forth to this rhythm. So as I was physically swaying to this bass and drum track, Karen asked me about the book under my arm. It was *Possessing the Secret of Joy* by Alice Walker, and it opened up the conversation to a practice with which I had been unfamiliar. It is now widely known as FGM, or female genital mutilation. How women behave toward each other within the global culture of patriarchy is the discussion that the song "Cornflake Girl" wanted to take part in.

Twenty-seven years from the inception of "Cornflake Girl," listeners continue to share with me their insights about the song. Someone confided that her mother tried to justify her controlling behavior toward her daughter by saying, "I'm only doing this because I love you." Over the years hundreds of letters and conversations have taught me the severity of the words "I'm only doing this . . ." In one letter, "doing this" was threatening to cut off communication and support unless the daughter agreed to what the mother wanted her to do.

In other letters the context was a severed friendship, possibly poisoned by outside influences. One woman wrote to tell me that a woman she cared for dearly was becoming more and more isolated and controlled by someone else. In this instance the letter writer was having a difficult time accepting that the isolated woman was defending the behavior of her manipulator.

The details of each story have varied over the years, but the feeling of deep betrayal is consistent with most interpretations of "Cornflake Girl."

"Doing this" can take on sinister implications. "I'm only doing this to save you from yourself." This story was told to me by someone who knew the two people involved and who asked, "When are the words 'tough love' an excuse for abuse?" At the center of the story was a mother and a daughter. The mother identified as a Christian. She believed that sex before marriage was a sin. The daughter's religious beliefs were not specified. Her grades were very good, and she was very involved in her high school. Apparently she had gotten birth control, believing it was the responsible thing to do. When her mother discovered the birth control hidden away somewhere, she tampered with it, without the daughter knowing.

The mother felt the daughter had to pay for her sin and wear her shame.

The daughter became pregnant and was "forced" to give birth.

The question is still valid: When is the justification of tough love actually just an excuse for abuse?

A song can help open my eyes to the many emotions surrounding a complex issue. When I enter "Cornflake Girl" as an energy, she demands that we talk about what women perpetrate on each other and what women withhold from each other. "Cornflake Girl" allows people into her frequency by being quite welcoming. I found her that way at first, anyway. The more I was bearing witness, through all kinds of scenarios, to women-on-women violence—and in the case of FGM, we have to talk about women-on-girl violence—the more I would burst out and say *This is not really happening,* and the answer I kept getting back was *You bet your life it is.*

FGM, female genital mutilation, is described by the World Health Organization as "procedures that involve partial or total removal of the external female genital organs for non-medical reasons." This is child abuse on a grand scale. Most girls affected by this harmful practice are cut between infancy and fifteen years of age.

The numbers are overwhelming. The United Nations Population Fund estimates that 200 million girls and women alive today have been subjected to FGM. More recent data suggest that 68 million girls will be cut between 2015 and 2030. It's estimated that 3.9 million girls were cut in 2015 alone. This number will increase to around 4.6 million a year if this abuse is not addressed globally.

The numbers continue to shock, revealing how many girls and women are at risk throughout the world, including in the United States and the United Kingdom. According to the Centers for Disease Control and Prevention, 500,000 women and girls living in the United States are either at risk for or have undergone FGM.

There are subjects songwriters take on because the subject haunts them. My view of this particular women's issue was pried open by Alice Walker's words. Years later I am still learning about the complexities surrounding this harrowing practice.

At first, I could not understand how someone could say they loved a young girl and then take her to a "cutter," who might use a razor blade, a scalpel, scissors, a knife, or a piece of glass to cut out a portion of or all of the girl's genitals. As I have been exposed to this practice and am still understanding more each day, it has become essential for me *not* to view it only as part of certain cultural communities. This is global gender inequality. If we do not get involved, the numbers of victims of FGM are set to rise.

With that in mind I began recently to research the origins of this violent practice and how we as women became complicit in it. Women and men are carrying on the tradition and taking their daughters to have their genitals cut, and health care officials, teachers, judges, and lawyers are also perpetuating this violence. Even if by turning and looking the other way, many people are culpable. We have to talk about this because it's not going away and no one in the United States has been convicted of the practice. Those involved must be held accountable. Are U.S. state lines being crossed to take girls to a medical care professional who is getting paid handsomely to violently abuse them?

FGM predates the rise of Christianity and Islam and has been practiced all over the world. So it is not the province of a single religion. As the United Nations Population Fund states on its website (UNFPA.org), "In Western Europe and the United States, clitoridectomy was described to be practiced so as to treat perceived ailments like hysteria, epilepsy, mental disorders, masturbation, nymphomania and melancholia in the 1950's."

The information on UNFPA.org is useful to those of us trying to understand the severity of and the complex psychological issues attached to this life-changing procedure. For families to stop cutting girls, they will need support from the wider community. Because FGM is a prerequisite for marriage in many communities, economic necessity justifies the practice to many parents. The narrative has also been cleverly controlled by the patriarchy. One unbelievable myth warns that an uncut clitoris will grow to the size of a penis, heaven forbid.

(The album that "Cornflake Girl" is on was originally entitled *God With a Big G*, but that got shot down by someone at the label. So then the Muses guided me to the more expansive album title *Under the Pink*. This reference was intended to speak to most women, who have a pink- to flesh-colored G-spot associated with their internal anatomy.)

Lies claiming that FGM will enhance fertility or ensure child survival are passed down through the generations. According to the United Nations Population Fund, many people believe that a woman's sexuality is "insatiable if parts of the genitalia, especially the clitoris, are not removed. [FGM] is thought to ensure virginity before marriage and fidelity afterward, and to increase male sexual pleasure." The patriarchy was able to get some women to agree that "the external female genitalia are considered dirty and ugly and [should be] removed . . . to promote hygiene and aesthetic appeal."

We can all become indoctrinated into a narrative that is harmful, a narrative that can have deadly consequences, a narrative that can scar a person for the rest of her life. Physically and psychologically scar a person for the rest of her life.

First and foremost we have to have compassion and understanding for the women who have been cut as girls and who, as women, still believe that in order to protect their daughters, they too must be cut. But the reality is that FGM is one of the worst forms of sexual assault. FGM is child abuse of the worst kind.

In response to the first conviction in the United Kingdom of a mother committing FGM on her three-year-old daughter, a woman has come forward to say that she could have easily been that mother. That she would have practiced FGM and cut her daughter had a health care professional not explained the harmful effects her beloved girl child would suffer. The woman had been cut herself as a girl and thought, Well, this was done to my grandmother, and then done to my mother, and then done to me, so if I don't continue the cultural tradition I will have failed them all, including my daughter.

The psychological torment of this practice is heartbreaking. Truly heartbreaking. In many cases, as it is linked to a rite of passage, the older women in the room (who may take part in the cutting by spreading the girl's legs and holding them down) defend it as tradition.

The result of this violent practice is for the girl to have no sexual desire. The result of continuing the practice of FGM is to subjugate women physically and psychologically. The result of all of this is the global control of a gender. Some of the defenders of the practice of FGM, usually downplaying it by calling it "circumcision," are very powerful religious leaders. Some religious scholars, however, have said that FGM is not in the holy books and that religious leaders are only voicing their opinion.

I encourage people to listen to survivors of FGM tell their stories. The telling of their stories is not just about educating us and informing us about this harmful practice. These women survivors are allowing us to feel the depth of their pain, not only physical but the additional heartache of trust dying in the harsh light of such a betrayal. These women are sharing their wounds, physical and emotional, and showing us how they have transformed and transmuted these wounds. These women are on a path of empowerment and healing through their activism.

They all say in their own way, "We were cut for men."

FGM activists are doing everything they can to make sure this abusive practice doesn't go underground. Survivors devoted to change are speaking out about what has been a closely guarded secret.

Listening to the women describe being terrified as they are held down, usually by people they have trusted, has had a searing impact on me. Each story is so deeply personal, with one woman intently detailing how the cutter had sawed away at her flesh, which the cutter then threw across the room. She was talking about her clitoris being sawed off, piece by piece, as she was screaming in pain, and then voicing her realization that this portion of herself has been *denied her*, discarded, thrown away, and was gone forever.

The journey from abuse to empowerment of Khadija Gbla, Dr. Isatou Touray, Jaha Dukureh, Halimatou Ceesay, Leyla Hussein, Rhobi Samwelly, Nimco Ali, and many more, each telling her story, is the testament of turning sexual assault and child abuse into powerful, meaningful, *effective* global activism.

CORNFLAKE GIRL

Never was a Cornflake Girl
thought that was a good solution
Hangin with the Raisin Girls
"She's" gone
to the other side
Givin us a yo heave ho
things are getting kind of gross
and I go at sleepy time
This is not really Happening
You Bet Your Life It Is
You Bet Your Life It Is
Honey, You bet your life
It's a
Peel out the Watchword just
Peel out the Watchword

she knows what's going on
seems we got a cheaper feel now
all the Sweeteaze are gone
Gone to the other side
with my Encyclopedia
They musta paid her a nice price
She's puttin on her string bean love

This Is Not Really Happening
You Bet Your Life It Is
Rabbit, where'd you put the keys girl
Rabbit, where'd you put the keys
RABBIT where'd you put the keys
where'd you put the keys girl?
and the Man with the golden gun
thinks he knows so much
thinks he knows
so much
and the man with the golden gun
thinks he knows
thinks he knows so much

I know you know I know it's not easy
I know you know I know it's not easy
Rabbit where'd you put the keys girl

REALIZING IN THE AUTUMN of 2001 that the song "Imagine" could be threatening was illuminating.

Dangerous songs mean something very different to dangerous men. Dangerous songs can gift a healing balm to the world, whereas dangerous men usually spread destruction and death. However, dangerous men are rarely in danger themselves—and those in the dangerous men's club reap huge profits because of this.

The people who warned me about how important it was for us, as a collective, to persist with the Strange Little Tour in 2001 were not wrong. This time in history was emotionally raw and explosive. On one hand, we Americans were having to process our shock, trauma, and grief from an unprecedented attack on our country; on the other hand, we were having to become quickly adept at deflection or risk being infected by a ferocious aggression coming almost daily from the Bush administration. In city after city, town after town, I was handed letters updating me on what was going on from each letter writer's perspective.

Every audience was a cross section of people with many different skills, insights, and access to information. As an artist on tour at this particular time in history, I was in a unique position to get a sense of what was going on in different cities, in different countries. At the time I could get this perspective only from being on the ground. It became apparent that people were coming to the shows to gather and exchange information. The set list of each show would reflect and synthesize what I had learned from my one-on-one conversations with my main source of intel: the audience. The consummate audience was not passive but actively collaborative, and because of their insight, the narrative of the show every single night was documenting this crazy historical time. Audience and artist were truly working together, joining minds and hearts through song choices during this emotional and mental collective crisis.

In just over three weeks we went from being a country under attack on September 11 to Bush announcing on October 7 the invasion of Afghanistan.

The day before October 7 I found my teenage self somewhere on M Street in Georgetown, Washington, D.C. She reminded me that I had played more nights and sung more songs in this city than in any other city in the world. She thought that touring during the country's seismic-off-the-scale emotional state, weaving a story through a different set list, was probably a very heavy energy to create with almost every night. I admitted to her I had never had to play to so many broken hearts before. The grief was at a level unknown to me before Strange Little Tour. My teenage self thought that embracing the fact that I had sown more song seeds here than anywhere else in the world could help ground me for the two D.C. shows. The need for grounding was critical in order to be able to listen to the songs that wanted to come forward on the evening of October 7.

Certain factors determine how, as an artist, you are going to respond to a massive historical moment such as your country going to War.

The first strikes on Afghanistan were announced from the White House before 1:00 p.m. local time.

Neither the audience nor the local crew missed the irony that we were playing at Daughters of the American Revolution Constitution Hall. My resistance to the Bush administration's manipulation of 9/11 truly began there. The set list from that night tells me everything I need to know about the emotional state of everyone in that room.

Before the show that night, fears were expressed to me backstage from fathers whose kids were going to be deployed in this war on terror. And although George W. Bush spoke about invading Afghanistan, the song "Sweet Dreams"—a song I had written about the Gulf War and George H. W. Bush ten years prior—demanded to be played that night. I also played a sinister version of the nursery rhyme "This Old Man," leading into the Slayer song "Raining Blood," the latter having been requested by someone whose son was going to war.

My call to action as an artist was not to utilize the magic of music for escapism. Not on that night. Yes, there are times when I consciously choose to wave music's magic wand so the audience can absolutely escape from reality, but not on October 7, 2001, and not on March 20, 2003, when we invaded another country and began another war.

Both set lists were reflective of the songs themselves stepping forward, as well as the audience demanding that our political class be held accountable for their abuse of power.

From October 7, 2001, onward, we have been a nation at war.

There were so many issues I did not understand at the time that have been revealed to us over the years.

I did not comprehend the scope of the imperial authoritarian agenda at the time. We as a country were being groomed to agree to a war that would make a few greedy men even richer. I did not process the level of corruption that would be revealed to us by fearless reporters when they exposed the practices of Halliburton and Big Oil and oh-so-many corrupt others as the months turned into years. But I did realize that with "Imagine," one of the most important songs ever written about the possibility of a peaceful world, not being part of the conversation meant that we were in ominous times. The thought of war and the marketing of war was the narrative all around us. And it was relentless.

This thought expanded itself to the wider public, including me, on January 29, 2002, when I heard President Bush's State of the Union address naming Iraq along with Iran and North Korea as countries he defined as an "Axis of Evil." There it was. Iraq.

SCARLET'S WALK

If you're a Thought
you will want me
to think you
and I did
invited a Guest
up until
you announced that
you had moved in

"what do you plan to do with all your freedom?"
the new sheriff said quite proud of his badge
"you must admit the land is now in good hands"
yes, time will tell that
you just lift your lamp

I will follow
Her on her path
Scarlet's Walk
through the violets
just tell your Gods for me
all debts are off this year
they're free to leave
yes. they're free to leave

leaving terra
leaving terra

there was a time
when I thought that
Her destiny
should have been mine
Big Brave Nation
but instead
her Medicine now
forgotten

"what do you plan to do with all your stories?"
the new sheriff said quite proud of his badge
we'll weave them through
'every rocket's red glare and huddled masses'
you just lift your lamp

I will follow
Her on her path
Scarlet's Walk
through the violets
just tell your Gods for me
all debts are off this year
they're free to leave
yes. they're free to leave

leaving terra
leaving terra

if you're a Thought
you will want me
to think you
and I did
and I did

FROM THEN ON, IT was clear that I was writing an album with a very different intention from what I had thought I would be writing. *Scarlet's Walk* would be a sonic pathway, taking a different road from that of the dangerous men, their road leading them to what seemed to be a premeditated war. There would be a map of Scarlet crossing the country as she discovered her spiritual connection to her other mother, America. Art would have to imitate life.

After January 29, 2002, all the pieces of the album began weaving themselves together. I began to hear the cohesion through the many songs' concert of ideas. The Muses were direct: *If you are a creator and you're creating work, you're going to have to create it to whatever is world-bending at THIS moment. Here is the world of global crisis; here is the artist potentially at the crisis because of that world crisis. You have your marching orders. Create and Go.*

We had just crossed the country on tour. I had lived a version of Scarlet's Journey. The songs had planted their seeds as we walked and drove across the country. They were intertwining—weaving old stories with new. Songs are an ancient, strange magic. If I chase them, they elude me; if I don't hunt for them I will miss details that will matter usually in the second verse or the bridge, and I have to earn their trust by doing my part. Day after day in the autumn of 2001, we had walked with and listened to people processing all the energies unfolding in real time. And at night we drove as the land moaned, unearthing her latent memories. With the physical invasion and desecration of the Twin Towers, emotions unknown to many of us were demanding to be dealt with.

A Native American woman asked me if I would trust my own mother's keeping in the hands of those who were declaring war at the time. And if not, why would I entrust our spiritual mother, America, into the hands of these men? She made it very clear that as an artist my dedication had to be to write toward the release of our spiritual mother from her political pimps. She explained to me that hundreds of years of suppressed voices were ready to speak. They were there to reveal past wounds and, by doing so, they would share their losses and their hopes—the lessons they had learned and their vision for our spiritual mother, America. Some stories and songs would be painful to hear, but in their way these songs and stories were a type of protection, a sonic salve for what had seemed an untreatable wound. These songs would have to penetrate through a patriarchal narrative of America that had been sold—and sold *hard* to some of us.

We were told the lie that Iraq had WMDs, weapons of mass destruction. We were told the lie that Saddam Hussein and Iraq were involved in 9/11. There was barely a mention of Saudi Arabia and the fact that fifteen of the nineteen terrorists had been Saudi Arabian. No, it was just a barrage of *Iraq. Iraq. Iraq.* The words "weapons of mass destruction" were repeated ad nauseam.

One rule of songwriting I have found to be useful is that to understand a present situation I find overwhelming, I have to follow a current narrative's thread to its tangled past.

PNAC (Project for the New American Century) was a neocon-
servative think tank founded in 1997 by William Kristol and Robert
Kagan. In 1998 it sent letters to President Bill Clinton advocating
for "the removal of Saddam Hussein's regime from power" in Iraq.
The signatories of these letters—among them, John Ellis "Jeb"
Bush, Dick Cheney, Donald Rumsfeld, and Paul Wolfowitz—
became closely associated with the war beginning in 2001 and with
the invasion of Iraq. In 2002 President George W. Bush and some
of those same signatories would justify the invasion of Iraq by referring to the Iraq Liberation Act, which passed the House and the
Senate in the autumn of 1998. On October 31, 1998, Clinton signed
the bill into law.

↯ ↯ ↯

In early August 1998, we were in Washington, D.C., on the Plugged
Tour supporting the album *From the Choirgirl Hotel*. A small group
of our party was given a private tour of the White House.

By then I had been married for just over five months, and as I
sat in that chair in the Oval Office that day, we were all aware of
the scandal swirling around the events that took place in that very
room. There were investigations concerning the affair of President
Clinton with the intern Monica Lewinsky. All kinds of sordid details
were being unmasked and put under microscopes by Kenneth Starr
and Brett Kavanaugh. It wouldn't be until over twenty years later
that, through YouTube, I would hear Lewinsky describing what
she had gone through in 1998. How in the office of the indepen-

dent counsel she had to authenticate all twenty hours of phone calls that had been taped by a friend. She talked about "the stealing of people's private words" and she talked about a public without compassion. She talked about Shame as an industry. She had lost her dignity and her reputation. And now she was reliving a time when her mother feared her daughter would literally be humiliated to death. She concluded, "It's time. It's time to take back my narrative."

Taking back narratives is important. It is part of a songwriter's commitment and oath to the Muses. After hearing Monica speak, I felt my mind drift back to the memory of being in the White House on that hot August day in 1998.

Sitting in the Oval Office that day, I thought about all the conversations that had happened there. All the decisions that had been made and that would be made—good or disastrous—in the future.

I thought of all the presidents and their first ladies. Of first ladies having to bear the consequences of their husbands' having affairs. As I was wondering about this, I started humming the song "Jackie's Strength." This song is about many things—birth, death, and marriage—a hugely personal song written before I got married on February 22, 1998.

I had heard all my life that people could remember where they were and what they were doing on Friday, November 22, 1963, the day they heard that JFK had been shot. In November 1963 my father was pastor to the Dumbarton United Methodist Church in Georgetown. On the Sunday following the assassination of President Kennedy, he took my sister and brother to see the president lying in state in the Rotunda of the Capitol. My sister can still recall that Monday sitting on the Arlington Memorial Bridge at six years of age as President Kennedy's casket passed her in a carriage pulled by horses whose manes seemed to touch the sky. I was three months old to the day when my mother, after hearing over the radio that JFK had been shot, put me down and said a prayer—and prayed for Jackie's Strength.

A song can link childhood and the political landscape of adulthood in just a few minutes.

JACKIE'S STRENGTH

a Bouvier

till her wedding day

shots rang out

the police came

mama layed me on

the front lawn

and prayed for Jackie's Strength

feeling old

by twenty-one

never thought

my day would come

my bridesmaids

getting laid

I pray for Jackie's Strength

make me laugh

say you know what you want

you said we were the real thing

so I show you some more and I learn

what black magic can do

make me laugh

say you know you can turn

me into the real thing

so I show you some more and I learn . . .

⟨ ⟩ ⟨

stickers licked on lunch boxes
worshipping David Cassidy
yeah I mooned him once
on Donna's box
she's still in recovery
sleepovers
Beene's got some pot
you're only popular
with anorexia
so I turn myself
inside out
in hope someone will see
we'll see

make me laugh
say you know what you want
you said we were the real thing
so I show you some more and I learn
what black magic can do
make me laugh
say you know you can turn
me into the real thing
so I show you some more
and I learn . . .

? ? ?

I got lost
on my wedding day
typical the police came
but virgins always get backstage
no matter what they've got to say
if you love enough
you'll lie a lot
guess they did in Camelot
mama's waiting on my front lawn
I pray
I pray
I pray for Jackie's Strength

THE THOUGHT OF A PERSON being silenced is scarily as relevant today, in 2020, as it was when the song "Silent All These Years" was written thirty years ago. At the time, the song showed me that there were outside forces that would deliberately try to silence people. And in that nefarious act of silencing us, we may lose our courage to speak up. And in doing so we would accomplish their censoring for them. If you or I mute ourselves, we have been threatened or shamed into silence. And once again the perpetrators, bullies, and predators steal and possess the narrative, claiming they are the real victims.

The art of silencing someone is a dark art, indeed.

"Silent All These Years" still is one of the most important songs to me personally. Without her, I would not be writing to you now. She was the life support that helped me survive a severe personal and artistic crisis.

In my mid-twenties, in the late '80s, these intersecting artistic and personal failures forced me to look at my life. I had to own the direction where some of my personal choices and my songwriting had taken me.

I somehow had managed to silence my inner magical child artist, the one that had taught me the love of music and the power of songs. The only way I got through this artistic death was by writing songs to survive it. Some of us have to go through a personal tragedy in order to find our True North as writers or songwriters. It took me four years to hear the Muses and my own voice to be able to write and record the songs that became the final version of the album *Little Earthquakes*. It was a long and arduous climb to song-write my way out of a very personal hell. "Silent" was not necessarily written to be a political call to action, but it became one, and I did not stop it. Women around me at the time saw the highly charged gender divide we were in during the autumn of 1991.

Me and a Gun, the EP, was about to be released in October 1991, and it included "Silent All These Years."

The Muses cautioned me, *You wrote songs personal to you. However, the issue of sexual assault is blowing up in the political world. The personal is political.*

On October 11, 1991, in her full opening statement, Anita Hill gave voice to being a survivor of sexual harassment. A woman of color, she faced a panel of fourteen white men on the Senate Judiciary Committee and said, "I could not keep silent."

"Silent All These Years" would speak to this. And so too would "Me and a Gun."

SILENT ALL THESE YEARS

Excuse me but can I be you for a while
My dog won't bite if you sit real still
I got the Anti-Christ in the kitchen
yellin' at me again
yeah, I can hear that
Been saved again by the garbage truck
I got something to say you know
but nothing comes
Yes I know what you think of me
you never shut up
yeah I can hear that

But what if I'm a mermaid
in these jeans of his
with her name still on it
hey but I don't care 'cause sometimes
I said sometimes I hear my voice
and it's been here
silent all these years

So you found a girl who thinks
really deep thoughts
What's so amazing about really deep thoughts

Boy you best pray that I bleed real soon
how's that thought for you

my scream got lost in a paper cup
You think there's a heaven where some screams have gone
I got 25 bucks and a cracker
do you think it's enough
to get us there

'cause what if I'm a mermaid
in these jeans of his
with her name still on it
hey but I don't care 'cause sometimes
I said sometimes I hear my voice
and it's been here
silent all these

years go by
will I still be waiting
for somebody else to understand
years go by if I'm stripped of my beauty
and the orange clouds raining in my head
years go by will I choke on my tears
'til finally there is nothing left
One more casualty
you know we're too easy easy easy

♩ ♩ ♩

well I love the way we communicate
your eyes focus on my funny lip shape
let's hear what you think of me now
but baby don't look up
the sky is falling
your mother shows up in a nasty dress
hmm it's your turn now
to stand where I stand
everybody lookin' at you
Here take hold of my hand
yeah I can hear them

But what if I'm a mermaid in these jeans of yours
    with her name still on it
hey but I don't care 'cause sometimes,
I said sometimes
I hear my voice
I hear my voice
I hear my voice
and it's been here
silent all these years
I've been here
silent all these
silent all these years

ME AND A GUN

Five a.m. Friday morning Thursday night far from sleep
I'm still up and driving can't go home obviously
So I'll just change direction 'cause they'll soon know where I live
And I want to live
Got a full tank and some chips
It was me
and a gun
and a man
on my back
and I sang "Holy Holy" as he buttoned down his pants
You can laugh
it's kind of funny
the things you think
in times like these
Like I haven't seen Barbados so I must get out of this
Yes I wore a slinky red thing
Does that mean I should spread
for you
your friends
your father
Mister Ed
it was me

and a gun

and a man

on my back

But I haven't seen Barbados so I must

get out of this

And I know what this means

me and Jesus a few years back

used to hang

and he said "It's your choice babe just remember

I don't think you'll be back in three days time so you
*   choose well"*

Tell me what's right

is it my right

to be on my stomach of Fred's Seville

it was me

and a gun

and a man

on my back

But I haven't seen Barbados so I must get out of this

And do you know Carolina

where the biscuits are soft and sweet

these things go through your head

when there's a man on your back

and you're pushed flat on your stomach

It's not a classic Cadillac

it was me
and a gun
and a man
on my back
But I haven't seen Barbados so I must
get out of this
no I haven't seen Barbados so I must
get out of this

A JUDGE CAME BACKSTAGE to see me in 2009. She spoke with me privately. First she spoke about a song that she had developed a relationship with that had been with her on her journey.

It has now been over ten years since she told me her story. And the reason it has stepped forward now is because I am hearing stories similar to hers, and more frequently. Which means as part of my creative process I am documenting what people are sharing with me at this time to create a song for the future album.

I don't know how this will play out, but I am beginning to make a web out of the impressions that are coming to me. For a long time I have written words and made simple drawings that interconnect. Not every element is utilized, but it's a way to grow and expand an idea. It can take the form of a map similar to the one in the artwork in the liner notes of *From the Choirgirl Hotel*. But it can also take the shape of a tarot spread or a medicine wheel or a family tree or a geometric shape.

This tool can be applied to any subject for any song. It's a mystery to me how the song will present herself. Research is an integral part of my writing process. Writing about an abusive relationship does not mean I only research abusive relationships.

I have a deep trust in the creative process that has proven to me over and over again that by utilizing these different web and map drawings the song is cocreating with me as we discover her potential together. I know how intersecting situations can propel a future work.

The judge had been living a life of torment and cover-up. She had what she considered "responsible power" in her courtroom, yet she felt powerless in her marriage as a victim of domestic violence. She cautioned me to never assume that a successful woman (or man) could not be suffering unthinkable abuse behind closed doors. Because a song I had cocreated had been with her through her abuse and subsequent recovery, she wanted me to understand the complexities she faced. She explained that the actual song had given her something and she wanted to give back.

I thanked her, saying, "We may be talking about a specific song that was with you through this nightmare, but while you are speaking seeds are being planted for future songs." She said she thought so.

She wanted me to comprehend her level of shame. She painted a picture of two very successful people having a good life. Looking in from the outside, some viewed her life with envy. They were invited to all the right functions, the exclusive parties, the charity galas, political fundraisers, openings for the ballet, art exhibitions, you name it. But as respectable as her place in her world was, her husband was extensively more powerful. She did not tell me when the abuse started or for how long she kept up the lie. But she said at a certain point she began to believe she was worthless, as he kept beating that thought into her. She believed she could not tell any of the people in her social circle as she was positive they would not risk getting involved and thereby making an enemy of her powerful husband. She began making friends with songs—one of them being mine—and these songs became her confidants. She had posed a question ten years earlier: Was domestic violence on the wane, or was it on the rise? And was predation pervasive within the judicial system, protected by the very people who interpret the laws? And silence people?

Within a few months of this conversation with the judge I was visited by a musicologist from the label Deutsche Grammophon. Dr. Alexander Buhr presented the idea of writing a song cycle based on classical themes. The sonic story began with a song I called "Shattering Sea."

SHATTERING SEA

that is not my blood on the bedroom floor
that is not the glass that I threw before
He gets his power from tide and wave
but grains of sand are my domain
His tempest surged an angry flash
then through my arms formed a sea of glass

Shattering Sea closing my eyes
Shattering Sea closing my eyes
Shattering Sea closing my eyes

every line
every curve
every twist
every turn
of every brutal word
every turn
every line
every twist
every line
every curve
every twist
every curve

resistance

of every brutal word
that is not my blood on the bedroom floor
that is not the glass that I threw before

LEFT: *Wedding cape*

BELOW: *Mark Hawley, Tori, and Rev. Martin Gillham*

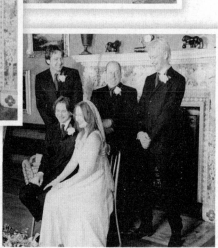

ABOVE: *Bridesmaids L to R: Karen Binns, Cody Dobyns, Llorraine Neithardt, and Nancy Shanks (Beenie)*

RIGHT: *Best men L to R: Rob van Tuin, John Witherspoon, and Marcel van Limbeek*

LEFT: *Johnny Witherspoon, 1992*

ABOVE RIGHT: *Kevyn Aucoin,
Tash, Mark, and Kevyn's dog*

ABOVE: *Live, 2002*

RIGHT: *Jenni Clark*

TOP LEFT: *Heading to stage, 2003*

TOP RIGHT: *Frozen on Promo in Scandinavia, 2005*

ABOVE: *Bosendorfer and Friends*

LEFT: *Mary, Ed, and Tori, Doll Posse Tour*

RIGHT: *Barry Lee Moe*

BELOW LEFT: *Moscow, 2014*

BELOW RIGHT:
Doll Posse Santa

BOTTOM: *Doll Posse Pip*

WHEN THE JUDGE SHARED her story with me, I was working on the album *Midwinter Graces*. We were recording over-dubs on the road, having finished basic tracking before the 2009 tour for *Abnormally Attracted to Sin* began. Therefore two albums were being created back to back in a very short time.

This is highly unusual for me, touring the release of a new album while creating another one at the same time. It meant I was coming out of a different recording studio somewhere in America fresh with *Midwinter Graces* playing in my head and then hearing people's impressions of other songs from past records and their stories associated with them—such as the judge. *Midwinter Graces* had a few original seasonal songs on it, but mostly it was made up of variations on themes of traditional carols. While the judge was speaking with me, John Philip Shenale's arrangements for the sixteenth-century "Coventry Carol" were layering a haunting dimension under her voice.

When Alexander Buhr approached me with his idea of a contemporary song cycle based on classical themes, we spoke in depth about *Midwinter Graces* and some of the discoveries the team and I had made together working with traditional carols. I applied to choosing carols the same technique that I had used before when recording a composition written by someone else, which is asking the song permission before I crawl into its structure, its sonic blueprint.

My experience has been that most songs are curious about different renderings of their essence. After working with them I say, *Thank you, Song, for showing me your secrets. Please work with me.* Or I thank the Song and admit that I do not possess certain energies or skills and another collaborator would serve them better and I respectfully leave their structure.

The process for one album can greatly influence another. *Midwinter Graces* acted as a guide as I began investigating how I would develop variations of classical themes for Deutsche Grammophon.

I believe that the judge's story helped to inform the protagonist in the song cycle *Night of Hunters*. At the heart of the narrative is a woman in crisis at the end of a relationship. The song cycle pieces together how the woman lost her self-worth. It was built in the bones of the story that a woman who saw herself as independent found herself trapped in a "grid of disempowerment"—which is also explored in "Job's Coffin," another song on the album.

The story was influenced by women as well as men who have survived abusive relationships and were willing to share with me the complex emotions evoked by verbal abuse and violent threats or both physical and verbal abuse they had experienced. People spoke with me about becoming a shell of their former selves. It became clear that with little to no self-confidence left, they felt they had very little ability to fight the oppressive controller in their life. All this needed to be explored in the narrative for the album. In order for the protagonist of the song cycle to regain her self-worth, she would have to go on a journey with the help of the spirit dimension. Her helpful companion takes the form of two animal familiars:

Anabelle, a fox, the hunter, and Anabelle, a goose, the hunted. The power of Nature was represented by the Fire Muse. Anabelle was voiced by Tash, and the Fire Muse was voiced by Kelsey Dobyns, my niece, continuing the collaboration after their involvement in *Midwinter Graces*.

Once I had the narrative loosely in place, my next challenge was pairing fragments of the story with classical themes. Not only did I express my anxiety to the collaborators on this project about "messing with the masters," as I termed it; I found myself sitting on the floor by the piano explaining my trepidation to all the dead composers. Many composers and their works were on my radar, so asking permission from each one became part of my daily ritual. The gratitude I have to the many composers who allowed me into their work is boundless.

And I truly believe that many of them are here in spirit to assist all of us to create by sharing the power of their art with us at this challenging time in our history. Their art documented humanity surviving cruelty and wars and it brought our ancestors great strength to survive grave injustices. The creators before us were called, and through music paintings sculpture poems songs stories and plays exorcised demons the way they knew how to—through their art.

The myth of Cerridwen (the goddess of poetry and transfiguration) and her potion inspired the song "The Chase" on the album. Cerridwen had two children: a beautiful daughter named Creirwy and a son defined as beyond outwardly hideous named Morfran. To give him a better future, Cerridwen, a very powerful "white witch" or "white goddess," decided to make a potion that would have to brew over a fire for a year and a day in a cauldron called Awen. The effect of the magic elixir would be to give her son such wisdom he would be revered by everyone. Cerridwen knew she had to protect what was in the cauldron because her power was well known. The fire was tended by a blind man, and Gwion Bach, a young boy, was to stir what was in the cauldron. After spilling three drops of the potion, burning his hand, the boy put his mouth on his burned skin. He had not known that the first three drops brought the gift of great wisdom and transfiguration, and the rest of what was in the cauldron would turn into poison. Cerridwen realized what had happened and began to chase him down as he transformed from one thing into another, thinking he could outsmart the white witch.

In *Night of Hunters*, Anabelle has been teaching the protagonist, Tori, how poetry can be weaponized by someone—possibly a poet who works for an evil lord who knows how to destroy someone through the wielding of words—and how it can have dangerous, devouring consequences.

In the ancient myth Cerridwen transformed herself into a hen after Gwion Bach had changed himself into a grain of corn. After ingesting this grain of corn she eventually gave birth to a baby boy. Instead of killing the baby she put him in a large pouch and tossed him into the sea, where he was discovered by fishermen and presented to a previously unlucky Prince Elffin. The baby boy was a prodigy and through his gift of poetry and prophecy became the legendary wizardly bard Taliesin. He had the power to inspire warriors to defeat invaders.

THE CHASE

(A duet between the protagonist called Tori
and the goose/fox Anabelle)

Tori: *Out there are Hunters*

Anabelle: *Let's say Predators*

Tori: *I have weapons that could destroy them*

Anabelle: *You must out create it's the only way*

I am the Hunter and the Hunted

joined together

Tori: *you create duality*

Anabelle: *and neutrality*

I must leave you with the Fire Muse

show her the riddle

It is serious if you lose

Out There

Tori: *I'll be the Hare*

Anabelle: *Then I'm the Greyhound*

chasing after you

Tori: *Then I'll change my frequency*

to a Fish that thinks

Anabelle: *Then you will find yourself*

in the paws of the Otter near her jaws

Tori: *Then I'll grow my wings as a Flying Thing*

Anabelle: *Flying Thing you be warned I'm the Falcon*

resistance

Tori: *Watch me change to a Grain of Corn*
Anabelle: *A Grain of Corn?????*
Hear the Alarm in your head?
I'm the Hen
Tori and Anabelle: *Black and Red*
Anabelle: *And You're in My Barn*
They would have won
Use your head
or you'll be Dead

WE DROVE PAST THE EXORCIST steps into Georgetown, which I recall as my beginning vision of our Pilgrimage in July 2016. I didn't know in the moment that one of the core tenets of my art for the next four years, and still as I write this, would be the exploration of the force "possession." I can't say that after four years of observing it and learning about it that I understand it. A person may believe in it or not, but I approach it as a force, and my experience of it convinces me that "possession" is a vast force.

Someone I have known for a few years wanted to tell me about their experience as a child. They are not of the Catholic religion, which has reported that exorcisms are on the rise. They said that they had been possessed by an evil spirit that was making them ill and that it was quite an ordeal for the spirit to be battled with and then expelled by someone we would term an exorcist.

Pilgrimage is a practice I have been applying as long as I can remember in order to jumpstart creativity. It really is a way to receive an electrical charge for a new project or a project whose battery needs to be recharged. This pilgrimage marked the beginning, and it made sense for several reasons in July 2016 to make the starting point Washington, D.C. This is the epicenter the candidates want to possess—the destination and all that comes with it if you are the next president of the United States.

My experience with possession is that although some of it feels destructive and malevolent, not all of it is. Based on everything people have confided to me or I have read about, I believe demonic possession is scary and life-threatening.

Another artist pressed me about the Muses, and the discussion we had pushed me to think about this in more depth. I maintained that what I shared with the Muses and the songs was a merging. And that is because I had seen the term "possession" as pejorative, referring to a demon taking over a human host. Whereas a "merging" was an agreement. The artist argued, "Look, T, if it walks like a duck and talks like a duck . . ."

"Maybe it's a goose?" I replied.

She said, "Call it what you want, but surely this deserves some investigating on your part—they are clearly related. Let me know what you find."

At the hotel in Georgetown, my sister, Marie, and I had met up with one of our dear friends, Polly Olsen from Yakama Nation. Polly and Marie were attending the conference being held in D.C. for the Association of American Indian Physicians, which Marie has been involved with for over forty years. In 1978 she attended the Indians into Medicine Program at the University of North Dakota, where she became copresident of the Association of Native American Medical Students. This is still an active mentoring program for AAIP.

Polly and Marie fired up the sage and sweetgrass and spoke about the importance of intention the night before I was to leave for the Smoky Mountains. First I had felt the pull to find the wonderment that my grandfather Poppa had for the mountains in the Deep

South. He had been a huge influence on me growing up, with his stories inspired by a Native American grandmother.

I also wanted to get a sense of how people were feeling. The Republican National Convention was in a week and the Democratic National Convention was in just a few weeks. Donald Trump would be the Republican nominee and the Democrats were divided between Hillary Clinton and Bernie Sanders.

Johnny—John Witherspoon, my friend and manager—and I left early. We wanted to get to Asheville, North Carolina, before sunset.

Pilgrimage is about breaking a pattern. Breaking patterns gets me to think in a different way. I am observing people in places I have not done so before. Because I am not familiar and "unconsciously safe," it's just a natural response that the volume on all my senses is turned up. The key is to balance the tension of calm documentation and the anxiety of the unknown. Yes, of course, this can also be the romanticism of the unknown. So I guess it's really balancing the romantic notions of a new situation and the people in them with the anxiety part of me that is ever watchful. All this for a song? Absolutely. Whatever it takes as long as those I love are okay.

Some writers create havoc in their own lives in order to bring this tension, which pushes them to a point that gives them new material. Trust me on this: there is new material out there and enough for all of us. Sometimes, though, I have found I have to take myself out of my routine to see it. A writer spoke with me about going to their writing place—a shed behind the house. This works for them. Another one I know has a houseboat so that they can stay there if the Muses appear. "And what happens when they don't appear?" a writer recently asked me. Indeed, most days I am *not* zapped by this magical force. Any form of writing is a discipline. Someone asked me how I handle writer's block. My response was that I do not subscribe to that notion. That is a vortex of writer's masochism I refuse to take part in. (Part of a songwriter's discipline is to be ruthless with lazy concepts.)

Going through my reference notes is proof that there has been a pattern of collecting ideas and then putting those ideas into an art form and releasing them into the world. So an input-output rotation. What about deadlines? Well, the truth is when I was an unknown artist no venue was being booked for me ahead of time. No one was waiting for my art. But for the past twenty years, my tours have been booked a year in advance, so I have to conjure *myself* if the Muses are busy visiting some other writer. There was a different pressure when I was an unknown artist: basic survival. But as a known artist you have to deliver on schedule. And over the years I have learned there are ways of achieving this. (To be clear, that is one of the reasons for writing this book.)

On a daily basis there are moments of taking ideas in and then forging them into art. It takes devotion and unrelenting discipline. All artists during a project will have to chop wood and carry water. Because songwriting can be such a loner occupation, it can be perceived as ephemeral. The problem with that is the actual distress in the letters I have received from demoralized writers, about how the reality of being an artist has been lied about. Talk about propaganda. And if I have been part of this, then I need to clarify.

Being an artist takes work, hard work. I didn't understand when someone in the boys' club in the music business would say "So-and-so had only one record in them." It took me a while to unpack this.

Writing the first record or the first book is not the hardest thing you will do. Writing the second or writing the sixteenth, possibly. That is because the writer will have had their whole life to write the first one. And most critics have a secret predilection for a virgin writer. There are too many writers right now who are depressed and forlorn, or just the opposite, in a state of panic that has pushed me to open anything and everything about my process to give them strength. Strength to fight the monster. Writing paralysis can be a monster. And the head games an artist plays with herself can be on the spectrum. To care so completely about reaching someone and at the same time staring back the void with a firm *Fuck you*—that is the tension we carry. No—that *I* carry. It's not fair to assume this particular process for all artists.

Back in the '90s, some critic asked me, "So, do you read your press?"

My response: "No. I weigh it."

She said, "How arrogant."

I looked her dead in the eye: "How sadistic."

This is a part of it all. It is not all faeries, Muses, and angels. Sometimes it feels like dancing with demons.

Being a songwriter is not always pretty. It can be scary because we are unearthing emotions that confront us with those portions of ourselves that we hide when posting on social media. The tension for me is holding the energy of service, to serve the song at all costs with a healthy dose of *Fuck off*. The piano seemed to say to me once, "Leave your pansy-ass self at the Thanksgiving table where it can serve you and keep you from arguing, but don't you dare bring it to me."

ƚ ƚ ƚ

By the time we got to Asheville, we had driven through a world I was not used to. No one batted an eye when a man with a gun on his belt ordered a skinny venti caramel macchiato with three extra shots. It hadn't taken us long after leaving Washington to begin to see pro-Trump bumper stickers.

We utilized the magical Asheville as a hub and then drove out early and arrived back for a late dinner. During this time we encountered all sorts of things. A tree was struck by lightning and branches fell on our windshield as Johnny was driving. We observed and listened particularly at lunchtime when we were far from a city center. People spoke of wanting change. We did get a sense that we were witnessing a mood that was not reflected in the potential voter polls. The sentiment among waitresses and waiters and fellow diners was that there was an *us* and a *them*. Those *so-and-so's* in Washington were all corrupt. How wannabe billionaires and real billionaires were going to change that, we weren't sure, but the point is there was a belief that billionaires were the answer to the problem. The masses had not bought that back in 1980, when, as I mentioned before, one of the Koch brothers was running for office on the Libertarian ticket. And that was because the billionaires were not hiding their philosophy at that time. They believed that a very few chosen people should have all the wealth and that you and I are worth only what we make. And when someone did some canvassing and realized that their true mission and message were not going down so well and people were not buying into signing on to serfdom, they did something so simple that it worked. They decided that in order to get people to vote against themselves and against their own welfare they would repackage their brand and lie about their true philosophy. Which was and is to have a small economic aristocracy and subjugate the masses, who will have to serve them under fiscal domination. They would buy politicians, lobbyists, and lawyers who would destroy democracy from within. There were also plenty of not-so-successful businessmen and businesswomen who were willing to do anything for their own gain. And something else was happening in July 2016. People felt empowerment through hate. Hate was possessing many people, from those in the GOP to the Dems to the Libertarians. It was across the board. We were living through a type of madness.

The spitting verbal venom took me back in time to a scene I had pushed aside. It had occurred twenty-one years earlier in the Deep South in the autumn of 1995. We were shooting the album art for my third studio album, *Boys for Pele*. The album had been recorded on both sides of the Atlantic, in a church in County Wicklow and in Kinsale, County Cork, in Ireland and then in the heart of New Orleans.

The location shoot was about two and a half hours from New

Orleans. Karen Binns, who is mixed-race, was naturally part of the team. She pulled me aside and said, "Tor, I am feeling really uneasy. People are giving me strange looks." At first I did not see it, I have to be honest. I told her, "They just have not seen your approach to London fashion."

But when we sat down to eat as a team and everybody's food came except Karen's, I started to take note. When it happened the second time there was no mistaking the hostility directed toward her. A comment was made about her when we were shooting in the middle of a burning field. *Send her back.* I confronted the man: "What the hell is going on?"

His justification? "You all chose to come here. Remember that."

As I write this about a time that I truly believed we had moved on from, the venomous chant "Send her back," which our own president has invoked, moves me to write a new song:

> *Send her back to Michigan*
> *Send her back to the Bronx*
> *Send her back*
> *Send her far away*
> *But what if that's the USA?*

I was born in North Carolina and used to spend many weeks a year there, so the South calls to me and holds memories. Taking a pilgrimage from D.C. to the Smoky Mountains in 2016 was taking on the feeling that we were again being guided by Scarlet, the main protagonist in the narrative for the album *Scarlet's Walk*.

At dinner in Asheville with welcoming college-age staff and a diverse group of diners, Johnny added to the story I had been sharing about the extreme treatment of Karen: her being embraced at restaurants in New Orleans and her abject unacceptance two and a half hours north of that city.

Johnny reminded me, "It wasn't just *Pele*. It happened in Montana during the shoot for *Scarlet's Walk*. I was there for that, as you may recall, and I had to ask about where her food was."

"Yes, it's all coming back to me," I said. "So what do you think that was about?"

He continued, "Well, the team included quite a few women from different cultures that were a powerful creative force and integrated. There was no sense of a hierarchy. There was no social ladder. Everyone was working together and voicing their opinions at the table. And our table was made up of people from various backgrounds."

"Okay. So we literally seemed foreign. Perhaps culture shock was being experienced from both perspectives." I was taking in his impression.

"Yeah, as a group we stood out. But do you remember that amazing encounter you had with the teenage lad?" Johnny asked me.

On one of the days of the shoot a teenage kid was watching us work from a distance, and after a while, when we took a break, he approached me. To paint the picture: We were in Big Sky country. Mother Nature is not oppressive in Montana; she brings the gift of expansion, not confinement. So when the young gay—closeted—kid confided what his life was like, the irony was not lost that his story was told under a limitless sky. But when any relationship except that between a man and a woman is seen as deviant, being an

LGBTQ person can be terrifying. Navigating dangerous waters was going to have to become his art form.

Perhaps because it was gay men who took me under their wing when I was thirteen and taught me how to survive—even at times through a large dose of reality, spelling out how a teenage girl in Washington could be manipulated—well, that's its own song, and those rivers run deep. Those fairy godfathers trying to teach me a drop of grace can go a long way, a lesson that my inner lioness needs reminding of a lot, but they gave and gave and gave and did not give up on me. Praise Jesus. So they led me, baptized in the barroom, to strength, to visibly blossom.

INVISIBLE BOY

you are
are not just
an invisible boy
if you want to be one
an invisible boy

you could go under cover
make your great escape
go where only eagles dare go
without needing wings
jump on a Triumph like Steve McQueen
it's time you lived your dream
"but how can this be" you say
"won't it all fade away
if I'm only made out of clay
only made out of clay"

you are
are not just
an invisible boy
if you want to reach her
as an invisible boy

z z z

you could sit down beside her
hold her as she cries
call upon your friends the cloud riders
to unlock the sky
then wave to the snowdrops skating by
catch the laughter from her eyes
"but how can this be" you say
"won't it all fade away
if I'm only made out of clay
only made out of clay"

you are
are not just
an invisible boy
if you want to be one
an invisible boy

you could cross over to the
Great Pub in the Sky
there you'll find him listening to a lost soul
pouring them a pint
then you'll know you have missed his advice
and he'll look you in the eye

"if you want to be" he'll say
"to be only partially a boy that's made out of clay
we're all made out of clay
but not you
you are my best invisible boy
if you want to be this
an invisible boy
then only those who can see you
will be better off because they can
see and believe in
my best invisible boy
my best invisible boy"

WITH A TOUCH OF Venus Envy, I surrendered to the Earth. She held some of the answers I was desperately seeking.

How does an artist document this particular time?

The next couple of days were spent in communion with Mother Nature as Johnny and I traveled through the Smokies, in many instances just taking in the energy. From Highlands to Franklin to Little Tennessee River we traveled. From Big Witch Tunnel in Cherokee we rode the ridges where we could be engulfed by Nature's spirit. From Black Mountain, North Carolina, lunching in Little Switzerland, passing Grandfather, Sugar Mountain, and Seven Devils, pausing at Green Knob, then through Blowing Rock, Nature was speaking and she did not relent. From breathtaking beauty and calm to a lashing and ferocious lightning storm, sometimes her creations wreak destruction. But she never destroys with malice—unlike us.

As we made our way to Wytheville, Virginia, the upcoming Old Fiddlers' Convention in Galax brought back a memory of a family tradition. As a little girl I was taken there every year. I would sit in the back with Mary as my dad drove and Uncle Woody rode shotgun, Camel cigarettes on the dashboard of the old burgundy Mercury.

In the late '60s and early '70s it was our tradition to go hear the fiddlers making their pilgrimage to a festival dedicated to Bluegrass. There were palm readers and all kinds of occult practices that Grandma Amos felt were a doorway for the devil's work. She also was not fond of music except for the Lord's glory. My Uncle Woody adored country music, and with a cigarette in one hand and a bottle of Miller in the other, he would walk through the camp where the fiddlers were warming up. I would follow him around as he went a-visitin' from campfire to campfire. "The stage," he would say, "is not where the real happening is, and don't let no one tell you no different, little niece. By that fire over there, now, you watch them cloggin' and keepin' time with them fiddlers. And see that gal over there? Probably made her way down from some hillbilly holler—yep, I reckon she'd be one a the best flat-footers you'll ever see. I swear you're wasting your time up there at that conservatory. You should be in these here mountains learning country music. And I do declare that if you listened to yer old Uncle Woody, one day maybe you'd meet Minnie Pearl and play at the Grand Ole Opry. Go on with ya now, and you can fry that bread up in the skillet and you mark my words it'll come to be."

Woodrow Amos, born June 30, 1924, enlisted and began his service in the 3rd Infantry Division. He served in North Africa, then took part in the Allied assault in Italy and eventually in Anzio, where he was wounded near his right eye. He almost lost that eye. He received a Purple Heart for this. After recovering in England, he was assigned to France and then Germany. He had trained as a medic and was known as "Little Doc." Not being an accredited medical doctor, he was never stationed in a field hospital. He would tell stories about being shot at on the field of battle while trying to keep a wounded infantry soldier from bleeding out. He made it clear that war was its own special hell. He couldn't say how many men he had lost or how many he had saved, but at a certain time of night, while the ashtray held a burning Camel cigarette, he would stand up, salute, and with reverence sing "Dogface Soldier" as a ballad with tears streaming down his face.

After Woody returned from the war, Grandma Amos—Addie, a missionary and teacher—wanted him to further his education. Woody chose a different path and reenlisted in February 1946, in the Army Air Corps, stationed at Denver and then at Merced, California. He served in the Korean War. Much later he was awarded the Bronze Star for meritorious service, having been wounded in battle assisting others. He spent much of his career in hardship posts where there was no doctor. If I remember right, he served at radar sites in Alaska, the Azores, and finally in Karamürsel, Turkey. During the Cold War the United States had a base there, not far from the Black Sea, where Russian radio transmissions of missile launches could be intercepted.

Woody didn't have a lot of time for religion, but he had been willing to die for his country. He told me there was nothing more important than to put your country first.

The seeds for the next album had been planted on that trip to the South, though it would take several months for those songs to step forward. Planting these songs in cities across America was the guidance I received from the Muses in the autumn of 2017. The questions that were being asked were about those with real power in Washington: Were their loyalties to their country first, or were any of them beholden to another country? Were they so compromised by a foreign country that they would betray America and all those who have fought and given their lives for the survival of our great republic?

We had toured Europe and the United Kingdom and were making our way across the states on the Native Invader Tour. We were repossessing words and concepts that had been invaded and then redefined. Words like "freedom" and "patriot" were a few on a long list that those opposed to democracy were trying to possess.

Making my way into Washington for the D.C. show, I remembered that hymn-like version of "Dogface Soldier" sung by Uncle Woodrow, a true patriot who was watching over me from his place in Arlington Cemetery.

RUSSIA

For those on the Right
you need to build a bridge
For those on the Left
you must build a bridge
For those in Washington
there is only one question
Is Stalin on your shoulder
Stalin on your shoulder
as he was with his composers

Time to wake
Activate our Native Invader
Warriors of the Earth
it's getting late now
Time to face
those who take more and more
from our Great Mother
the Mother we call home
Is Stalin on your shoulder

BARONS OF SUBURBIA

Barons of suburbia
take another piece of my good graces
I'm in my war you're in yours
do we fight for peace
as they take another piece of us
But baby I would let your darkness invade me
you could maybe turn this white light into navy
before you leave
It was a slight miscalculation
that my friends
my friends would be waiting
on the other side of the bridge
on the other side of this
This mole hill of a mountain
This potion now a poison
They're on the other side of right
We're on the other side of her midnight

When it's all said and done
we will lose a piece to a carnivorous vegetarian
Barons of suburbia
I have heard you pray before you
devour her

So baby will you let my darkness invade you
you always liked your wafer sweet
in the middle
before you leave

It was a slight miscalculation
that our friends
our friends would be waiting
on the other side of the bridge
on the other side of this
This mole hill of a mountain
This potion now a poison
They're on the other side of right
We're on the other side
of her midnight
I am piecing a potion
To combat your poison
I am piecing a potion
To combat your poison
I am piecing a potion
To combat your poison
I am piecing a potion
To combat your poison
I am piecing a potion
To combat your poison
I am piecing a potion

To combat your poison
I am piecing a potion
To combat your poison
She is risen
She is risen
boys
I said
She is risen

"BARONS OF SUBURBIA" was written out of anger directed specifically toward corrupt people in my life who were in positions of power. It certainly was not the first time anger had generated the energy that would then create a song response to diabolical behavior. Anger can be dangerous to create with because it can consume, and when it does, I become anger's embittered vessel. There are more than a few of those songs in my song graveyard.

But focused anger can be converted into an inner fire that can give an artist the stamina she will need to do the research necessary to write the songs, record the songs, mix them with the team, and then tour them live.

Defiant activation with passion for illumination has served me as a creator before, and this force has shown itself today as we begin to develop the new album to be released before the 2020 presidential election. Creativity is a Force that seems to know how to motivate its scribes and troubadours. The warning I heard today from the songs that have begun to form was "No one is going to save you, so you must save yourself. No one person is going to fight your battle for you. You must fight it yourself. Others will fight for Democracy's Life, too, but because you are not these people and you do not have their skills, only they can fight from their perspective and achieve liberation from Tyranny. You cannot create with their know-how, and they cannot create with yours. Pull yourself out of 'looking for a savior' syndrome and do your part. Others are being called to apply their powers to this battle for our Nation's Democracy. We are at a terrifying crossroads in our nation's history; therefore all artists need to be encouraged to value their unique experience. We will not relent."

YO GEORGE

I salute to you Commander
and I sneeze
'Cause I have now an allergy
to your policies it seems

Where have we gone wrong America?
Mr. Lincoln we can't seem
to find you anywhere out of the millions
from the deserts to the mountains
over prairies
to the shores
Is this just the Madness of King George
Yo George
Is this just the Madness of King George
Yo George
Well, you have the whole Nation
on all fours

EXPLORING CORRUPTION and psychological warfare in the new songs challenges me to approach the piano with gladiatorial containment. No, this is not the first time we have seen blatant corruption by those in our government—and it will certainly not be the first time I have written about it. But under the Trump administration there are unique strands to this tale that investigative journalists have been uncovering—strands that oppressors and tyrants will try to hide or bury. Every day political writers are enduring death threats while others have been killed for hunting down and revealing to us what is real and what is true. They have been warning that any of us can be targeted and have our thinking changed by political technologists. Some of them have been screaming for a while now that most of us can be groomed by the Russians and not even know it.

We are now not only having to confront the orchestrated attacks by outside enemy forces working diligently to upend our whole political system; we are having to admit that there are enemies of America—some of whom are Americans—who are willing to destroy our democracy for blood money.

The diligence of these writers and journalists has brought us precious facts. Recently I have been listening to two badass specialists on authoritarianism, Andrea Chalupa and Sarah Kendzior at Gaslit Nation, who demand that we shield ourselves from lies by arming ourselves with knowledge and that we can do that without waiting for a report. *The Road to Unfreedom: Russia, Europe, America* by Timothy Snyder, Craig Unger's *House of Trump, House of Putin: The Untold Story of Donald Trump and the Russian Mafia*, or Michael Isikoff and David Corn's *Russian Roulette: The Inside Story of Putin's War on America and the Election of Donald Trump*—all these informative works ignite the power of the written word to fuel any artist and their instrument, be it a Bösendorfer built from trees from an Austrian forest or a bass player's wooden wife. (At some point every musician's instrument has to become their significant other.) And right now this unprecedented crisis may require an artist to put her instrument above all else—day and night and for as long as it takes to serve the urgent messages and the Muses.

But first I must confess that after reading these works that explain in harrowing detail how we got to where we are and why we are in such a divisive, verbal-assaulting, word-twisting world where dictators and those who want to be dictators are winning the battle, I had to sit down. In the moment I didn't see this as being conflicted. Part of my process as an artist is that I can be sparked with ideas yet at the same time feel completely overwhelmed by what I have learned— while also *at the same time* trying to figure out how I am going to turn the information and the emotions surrounding the issues into songs.

When I am overwhelmed there is a blueprint that I faithfully follow: as a prosecutor follows the money, I follow the songs I trust with my life. Also, I trust the set lists from the live shows to be a mirror—my documentation of that city on that day—to give me historical context and not a whitewashed past.

Unlike some tours that are conceived months and months before their audience experiences them, my set list changes every day with the specific agenda to call out what is going on that matters to the people in that city that day. People pass me messages through other people if they can't show up at the meet-and-greet, explaining issues I might not know about, which continues to keep the shows as up to date and relevant as possible. The goal is to make each night a collaborative statement that cannot be erased because the set list is a time capsule in itself and tells me everything I need to remember about that day. Sound check does not begin until around 4:30 p.m., so the set list probably is not decided until 7:00 for an 8:20 curtain. However, it is absolutely imperative that I tell the story as best I can, so I have been known to make changes at the monitor board, in the area I call monitor city, where the crew is notified over their radio headsets seconds before I take the stage. Each song has a role to play, a purpose, and over the years certain songs have been known to repurpose themselves in order to make their point for that show that night.

TAXI RIDE

Lily is dancing on the table
we've all been pushed too far
I guess on days like this
you know who your friends are
just another dead fag to you that's all
just another light missing
on a long taxi ride

and I'm down to your last cigarette
and this "we are one" crap
as you're invading
this thing you call Love
she smiles way too much but
I'm glad you're on my side sure
I'm glad you're on my side still

you think you deserve a trust fund
just because you want one
sure you talk the talk when you need to
I fear the whole world is starting to
believe you

just another dead fag to you that's all
just another light missing

in a long taxi line
and I'm down to your last cigarette
and this "we are one" crap
as you're invading
this thing you call Love
she smiles way too much but
I'm glad you're on my side sure
I'm glad you're on my side still

Lily is dancing on the table
we have all been pushed too far today
even a glamorous Bitch can be in need
this is where you know
the honey from the killer bees
I'm glad you're on my side sure
I'm glad you're on my side still
got a long taxi ride ahead
got a long taxi ride
from St. Pete's
to Moscow
then back to Washington

June 15, 2014. Moscow, Russia

I was aware that our protest narrative would need to be fully grounded in the Crocus Arena the night before Vladimir Putin would take the same stage the next day.

The set list needed to reflect everything I had been learning from the Russian people over the years through conversations and letters. I am always amazed how some of them deal with propaganda and lies on a daily basis. Psychological warfare is a constant attack they must resist so they don't become completely demoralized or, worse, a convert or an unknowing messenger of the attacker, passing lies to someone who trusts them.

It's been drummed into my soul by those with this type of life experience that you either combat Kremlin disinformation or you become their asset, even defending to yourself why you are searching for enemies among your colleagues, family, and then even among your good friends. Westerners, when are we going to get this? Putin wants to resurrect a variation of the former brutal Soviet Union. With a gaggle of oligarchs served by presidents worldwide, including American senators and judges, to a name a few, Putin intends to be the head of a new global order. He believes America and democracy in any republic must be not just destroyed but annihilated from within. He believes most of us can be compromised by what we won't see sitting in our "blind spot."

Good people can be groomed. All of us are bait. No, some of us can't be bought with money, but every one of us wants something, even if it is to help someone we love. (If we can ask ourselves a very serious and important question—How can I be compromised?—*this* question is worth the beginning of a discussion with ourselves and with each other. Jesus, it might become a theme running through the new album.)

Over the years, Russians have confided in me how they defend themselves against this dark art of information warfare and one of its deadly symptoms—demotivation. Literally, the Russian people defend and armor themselves with art. The art they collect becomes part of their arsenal. It could be a passage in a novel they have memorized, one they have hard-wired in their mind. It could be the pattern in a painting that gives them a new vision. It may be that a poet has been able to reclaim words that have been infected by those who are weaponizing language and this poem has redeemed the words and transmuted them safe and sound back to the listener's arsenal. It might be a piece of music that resurrects an emotion the listener thought had been killed off. Any of the artistic disciplines could bring protection and resurrection. But the key was that they understood this and they believed it with every cell of their being. And that is what kept their hearts and minds free from imprisonment by tyrants.

That night in Moscow the set list also needed to include the perspective from the Ukrainian people, who had come to Russia to enlighten me about the battle they were waging for their country's future.

It was announced on June 13 that we would not be going to Kyiv: the show had been canceled by the promoter.

Just a few months earlier, on February 24, 2014, Russia had invaded Ukraine.

Since November 2013 Ukrainians, wanting closer ties with Europe, had been protesting President Viktor Yanukovych's pro-Moscow policies. He refused to sign a political association agreement and a trade pact with the European Union. Instead he accepted a deal from Putin, bringing Ukraine closer to a Moscow-driven Eurasia than to democratic Europe. Ukrainians took to the streets, calling this act by Yanukovych treason, which brought about Euromaidan and the Ukrainian Revolution. Antigovernment demonstrations continued in Kyiv, as did the violence against the protesters.

February 20, 2014, was Kyiv's worst day of violence, during which dozens and dozens of people were killed by sniper fire. Yanukovych fled to Moscow.

The meet-and-greet in Moscow on June 15 was very emotional for me. We had played St. Petersburg the night before, and I had been reading the many letters I had received there. My goal was to be better informed so I would ask useful questions at the Moscow meet-and-greet. But something magical happened, something that I have seen only once in a while over the years. The audience came up with the questions I should be asking and then enlightened me with their responses.

I have found there is no greater value than hearing about someone's own experience. How they see the world and why they see it the way they do. Then they usually point me in the direction of an article or a book or a documentary that expands on the subject.

Being in Russia at this particular time in history was a turning point for me as a person and as an artist. A year before, in June 2013, Putin had signed the "gay propaganda" law. It banned the "promotion of nontraditional sexual relations to minors." The consequence of this draconian law was that LGBTQ youth in Russia had very little access to health and educational support services about gender and sexuality. It affected teachers and psychologists, who now couldn't provide positive counseling. It was against the law to tell an LGBTQ teenager they were normal and provide them with reliable information about gender identity and sexual orientation. LGBTQ youth couldn't be directed to websites that understood the issues they faced. This federal ban included information provided by radio, television, press, and the internet. The persecution of the LGBTQ community was—and is—real and terrifying.

My set list in Moscow would speak loud and clear. There were requests, and someone brought me the lyrics to the lesbian anthem "Not Gonna Get Us" by t.A.T.u.

President Putin was scheduled to speak in the Crocus Arena the next day. But tonight the stage was not his. And the songs, the piano, the Muses, and I were going to serve the people who had in some cases risked a lot to get to this show in Moscow.

The set list was supposed to be as follows:

PART ONE
Parasol
Caught a Lite Sneeze
Tori Says Hello

Crucify

Bells for Her
Icicle
Purple People
Carbon
Weatherman

Lizard Lounge

Not Gonna Get Us
Love Song

PART TWO
Taxi Ride
Cooling
A Sorta Fairytale
Forest of Glass
Blood Roses
Take to the Sky

Encore

Cornflake Girl
In Your Room
Northern Lad
Hey Jupiter

The audience understood the energy. They were communicating mind to mind, heart to heart. The song "Carbon" was swapped out for "Leather" because the latter just burst through and took over at the piano, and when the songs do that I follow their lead.

"Not Gonna Get Us" into "Love Song" into "Taxi Ride" was a Call to Action, a sonic triptych.

But soon after that something very strange happened at the side of the stage, where Marcel van Limbeek sat at his monitor board. There was a lot of commotion.

When I walked off before the encore, more than a dozen very tall and intimidating men in suits were invading the stage.

They would later walk through all the rooms backstage, making sure that everything was secure for the next day, which really could have been done after I left.

But that was fine; I stood as they looked through my dressing room, politely standing my ground with the treasured letters I had been given by people from Russia and Ukraine safely in my handbag and coming with me.

First I would finish this protest show for the people who had come. We would not be bullied by intimidating security. I had not surrendered Crocus to them. Not yet.

As the crowd made its way to the front of the stage for the encore with hearts and minds and the most beautiful flowers, I told Mindi Pelletier, my very brave lesbian tour manager, to tell Andy Yates in monitor city to get on the radio and tell the crew another change was coming—and so was Anastasia.

/ / /

After the Moscow show we flew to Turkey. Luggage was collected and put into vans as we were put into SUVs, hugging the Bosporus on our way to the hotel in Istanbul, where we were staying after the Russia gigs. The letters from Russia and Ukraine were safe in my bags. Because Kyiv had been canceled, the crew had gone on to Bulgaria to wait for our show there, which in crewspeak means *Find an Irish bar*. The crew swears that wherever you are you can find an Irish bar and that you will be welcomed, swap stories, and enjoy a few pints.

The Mindinator (Mindi) made it very clear to me and to Barry Lee Moe (hair and makeup on the road and my gay confidant) that we could not run around Istanbul thinking we were in Paris.

So here was my problem: Not so many years earlier, I had run around Istanbul as if it were Paris with my new Turkish gal pals, who sought bargain prices for antique rugs. Istanbul reminded me of a variation on some of the stunning fashionable cultural cities in Europe. Afterward we would share the best mezze platter and tea on the Bosporus, and they spoke of their ambition and their goals as independent women. I found their ideas irresistible. There was a budding democratic energy percolating through the whole city.

This was gone now under the rule of Prime Minister and soon to be President Erdogan. Freedoms can be taken away before you realize they are gone.

Confined to my hotel, I traveled back through those memories. I looked around poolside and saw mostly women tourists ordering their lunch from waiters. The men were out and about doing business.

In 2005 I had been out and about doing all kinds of business, accompanied by amazing women in a progressive Turkish posse. These women worked in the entertainment industry, with the promoter, or with the record label. They spoke their minds about issues in their culture, about their personal and professional contributions as women to their society, and there was no fear of doing that back then. Turkey was modernizing and breaking the chains of draconian authoritarianism.

The concert I was to play in 2005 reflected what the stylish, innovative Turkish people were teaching me. And yes, this included going to the Blue Mosque, the Süleymaniye Mosque, and Hagia Sophia, which had been built in AD 537.

This set list was to reflect my newfound passion for this city that bridged Europe and Asia. It was a magical night for me, playing outside under the stars.

As I sat poolside in 2014, the memory of how that show ended hit me like a flare distress signal. Sometimes when things happen during shows, I soldier on and don't process what is happening in the moment. If I were to do that I might never finish a show or take a stage again. That's how I can keep doing this for forty years. To deflect crisis management to another time is how I cope with the strange and weird and even scary stuff that can happen on tour.

But as I sat in that four-star Turkish hotel under the sun, the final portion of that show in Istanbul played in slow motion. During the song "The Beekeeper," as I reached for the organ, I was thrown back into the Bösendorfer. I had never experienced an electric shock before, so when Marcel ran out to check on me, for a moment I didn't know what was happening.

Everything stopped and everything was still going all at once. I saw it as a warning—but a warning of what? Events tend to reveal—maybe even years later—the possible poetry of what seem like unrelated moments. A potential experience captured in a Polaroid, then filed in a time machine to uncover those layers later with the help of history's lens.

Hours after the outdoor concert on June 22, I thought how different the atmosphere was between the two Istanbul gigs of 2005 and 2014.

Someone working the 2014 Istanbul show had confided in me the real threats he faced as a gay man; these threats were getting worse by the year. The psychological toll it was taking led him to develop a disguise to protect him from being targeted. He spoke about the number of people like him in Turkey feeling the necessity to live double lives in order to keep their jobs. He told me that was why it was so important for supporters of LGBTQ rights to join together to promote equality at Istanbul's Pride, the largest LGBTQ celebration in the Muslim world. They did not know it yet, but some peaceful activists and supporters at Pride 2014 would be met with rubber bullets and tear gas. Watching a different country from your own become possessed by authoritarians who at their head have a tyrant or a mob boss, whatever you want to call it—this was not an unemotional observation.

The letters from Russia and Ukraine that I read over those few days in Turkey were a warning of a global economic aristocracy on the rise. Russia's people had been left with very little, while a few men got extremely rich. The letters explained that people had to be careful about what they said.

It was not as if thousands of Russians had not protested against the abuses of those in power. But many who did protest were killed or jailed. Others were threatened in other ways. Some said all this could never happen in America. Oligarchs . . .

But I had played piano bar off the K Street corridor in the late '70s and early '80s, underscoring that hotbed of conservatives. Yes, I was underneath them with my hands on the keys and my ears pricked. They thought a teenage girl was just a thing, serving their needs and playing their requests. The truth is, as I sat there playing what they wanted me to play I was listening to them as hard as I could and recording in my mind their every word.

YES, ANASTASIA

I know what you want
the magpies have come
if you know me so well
then tell me which hand I use
make them go
make them go

Saw her there in a restaurant
Poppy don't go
I know your mother's a good one
but Poppy don't go
I'll take you home
Show me the things I been missin'
show me the ways I forgot to be speaking
show me the ways to get back to
the garden
show me the ways to get around the get around
show me the ways to——
button up
buttons that have forgotten they're buttons
well we can't have that forgetting that
girls
girls

what have we done
what have we done to ourselves
driving on the vine
over clotheslines "but officer I saw the sign"
thought I'd been through this in 1919
counting the tears of ten thousand men
and gathered them all but my feet are slipping
there's something we left on the windowsill
there's something we left yes
we'll see how brave you are
we'll see how fast you'll be running
we'll see how brave you are
yes, Anastasia
and all your dollies have friends

thought she deserved no less than she'd give
well happy birthday her blood's on my hands
it's kind of a shame 'cause I did like that dress
it's funny the things that you find in the rain
the things that you find
in the mall and in the date-mines
in the knot still in her hair
on the bus I'm on my way down
on my way down
all the girls seem to be there
we'll see how brave you are

resistance

we'll see how fast you'll be running
we'll see how brave you are
yes, Anastasia
come along now little darlin'
come along now with me
come along now little darlin'
we'll see how brave you are

Memorial Day, 2019

There were fewer MAGA hats than I thought there would be.

Tash too observed this as we were setting up our folding chairs on the sidewalk in Stuart, Florida, to watch the Memorial Day parade, which would be made up of veterans and groups supporting them.

The piper gets me every time. Tash was focused on the Vietnam vets as they rode past, a few on their motorbikes. This is not something you see or that is talked about much in England, where Tash goes to school. There, the understanding of this war and the culture around it comes from films or documentaries and, of course, the music.

I remember the music. And I never get tired of hearing it or feeling the complex energies preserved in these amazing songs. From the dreamers writing to invoke a less violent world to the songwriters with their raw confrontations and the poets who would not let us look away.

The social revolution of the '60s was powered by music—by the songs that tore down tyrannical thinking and inspired people in grass-roots movements in local towns and cities to protest at the doorsteps of the Capitol and raise their voices within hearing of the White House. Songs were being written to rattle and shake the planet, to wake and fulfill the prophecy: "A Hard Rain's A-Gonna

Fall" and "A Change Is Gonna Come." And yes, it did. And many sacrificed their lives in the process.

The Vietnam vets passed us in bandanas and leather vests with screaming eagles etched on their backs, riding toward the gathering of veterans and their families for the service being held outside.

There we found Ed, our dad and grandfather, with his World War II cap on. He has never missed a Memorial Day service; usually he goes to Arlington Cemetery to honor his brother Woodrow, who is buried there. He had told Marie, my sister, the night before that he didn't feel able to come to the service. It had now been two weeks since Mary had died.

But the ladies who look after him and who had looked after Mary for two years were worried about him and believed he needed to get out of the house. And there he was, sitting in his chair waiting for the service to begin.

It hit me that people with very different points of view—whether religious, spiritual, or political—were all deeply affected by the men and women who had served our country and those currently in uniform. And there was a need to be there. Yes, it was very hot in that Florida sun, but no one was willing to leave until every wreath was laid.

A number of people spoke, but one woman's words won't leave me. Those words had an impact on everyone sitting in that sun.

She was there to honor her brother. He had served for several years before being killed in Afghanistan. She talked about the impact on his family, leaving children behind, and about the grief her whole family had to endure because of how much they loved him.

She reminded us that "freedom isn't free" and said that her family understood this on every level because they "had to pay the bill that day."

After the service, someone mentioned that soon it would be seventy-five years since the D-Day landings in 1944.

Once we were home, we began to talk about those in our family who had served their country and some of the stories they had shared that had been passed down.

Part of the need to share certain stories at certain times is that they help us to escape into an alternate world that for a short time takes us away from the reality of other stories that are just too painful to bear in that moment. The reality of Mary's death was overwhelming for everyone in that room: my sister, Marie; Tash, who had lost both her grandmothers within five months of each other; me, who had been wearing a mask to get through the past two weeks; Dad, who was showing signs of broken heart syndrome.

But he would allow himself to journey back in time through stories and songs, and he did have a fascination with the history and the stories of those who had been affected by the Great War and by World War II.

NOT THE RED BARON

Not the Red Baron
not Charlie Brown
think I got the message figured
another pilot down
and are there devils with halos
in beautiful capes
taking them into the flames
taking them
into the flames
not Judy G.
not Jean
Jean with a hallowed heart
I see that screen go
down in the flames
with every step with every beautiful heel
pointed

not the Red Baron I'm sure
not Charlie's wonderful dog
not anyone I really know
just another pilot down
maybe I'll just sing him a last
little sound

many there know some girls with
red ribbons
the prettiest
red
ribbons

IN LONDON AT THE END of July 2008 the crew and I boarded the Eurostar, which would drop us off in Lille, France. We were headed to play a concert in the city of Dranouter (previously Dranoutre) in Flanders, where so many soldiers had lost their lives in World War I. In that war alone, 10 million soldiers and 7 million civilians died. Dranoutre Military Cemetery, then, is a sacred place.

For me the process of understanding the history of a place can determine what I play. There are places I have played that demand that I do the research and find the stories that are forever emanating from them. But playing so close to a military graveyard was not something I had experience with, so I had to improvise. This began with my asking others about the war—and listening intently to them. Yes, sometimes the stories that motivate a song or a show come from strangers, but there are times when the stories are so close, such a part of the spiritual furniture of those in your life that you don't see them until some intersecting moment demands that you do. As we pulled out from St. Pancras station, my husband, Mark, and my manager, Johnny, also began to remember.

George Mann, Mark's granddad, was under seventeen when he joined the British army in 1914. His regiment was the Northumberland Fusiliers. Early in the war, Private G. Mann 55390 and others in his unit were hit by a landmine blast, which caused him to be deaf in one ear. Mark believes that only his granddad and the commanding officer survived the blast. George was then kept as a prisoner of war by the Germans for a few years.

He had been a fisherman for over twenty years when World War II broke out. As he was deaf in one ear and relatively old, he was not exactly the British navy's first pick. But by the end of May 1940, with help from their Panzer corps, the Nazis had trapped and surrounded the Belgian and French forces and pretty much the entire British Expeditionary Force, which convinced Winston Churchill that "the whole root and core and brain of the British Army" were about to be captured or killed on the beaches of France. This defeat would leave Britain almost defenseless in a likely German invasion. So George set sail in his fishing boat and along with over eight hundred other fishing boats, merchant boats, and small craft vessels picked up thousands of stranded soldiers at Dunkirk and other beaches in the north of France during Operation Dynamo and Operation Ariel and brought them back to safety.

Before going back home after being away for at least three weeks, not having told Rosa, his wife, that he was joining a flotilla of boats to evacuate soldiers from the coast of France, he joined the British navy as a minesweeper in the coastal command. He *did* know something about mines.

Johnny had five great-uncles, all originally from Liverpool, who fought on the Western Front. One of the brothers, Tom, had emigrated to Australia in 1910. In 1916 he joined the Australian Imperial Force and was assigned to the 1st Australian Tunneling Company, joining the battle at Hill 60 in Ypres. There on the field of battle, two of the other four brothers, all from the King's Battalion (Liverpool), found themselves face to face with their long-lost brother from Australia, serving with the many soldiers from the Commonwealth.

All five brothers survived the war, although they all suffered wounds or the effects of Yellow Cross, also known as mustard gas. One of the brothers, Michael, though badly gassed, died some years later, age fifty-two. Tom was wounded at Hooge Crater dugout in Belgium in 1917, but he made it back to Sydney at the end of the war. The oldest brother, Joseph, was severely wounded and died in 1936, eighteen years after the reunion at Hill 60.

Some in 1914 thought it would be a short war. Kaiser Wilhelm II of Germany assured his troops that they would be "home before the leaves fall." Instead, there was a Race to the Sea, *La course à la mer*, to envelop the northern flank of the opposing army; both sides dug in around the line attempting to win a war of attrition by grinding each other down physically and psychologically to the point of collapse.

So many losses. So many sacrifices. As I stood at the military graveyard, the song "1000 Oceans" was what I sang to the spirits of the fallen. My plan was to play it that night, but I didn't know if I would be able to hold that emotional line . . .

Words written in a wasteland of war by a Canadian soldier acted as a poetic torch leading me to the piano . . . and the poppies still do grow in Flanders Fields.

MARY'S RAVEN

no haunting whip-poor-will
gone is the meadowlark
calling to Mary's Raven
near and far
no robin's evening song
no pipers on that sand
will Mary's Raven guide me
through this nightland

BEFORE THE FARMERS ARE up and an hour or so after every single weary reveler has surrendered to the Sandman, there is quiet—a relief from outside noise. No cars on the road, no speedboats on the river, no tractors making hay while the sun shines—so here I am. Desperately trying to hear a message from the universe.

My mother, Mary, died May 11, 2019, two days after my dear friend Nancy—whom I call Beenie—died and a day before Mother's Day. Two women who taught me many things, two people who inspired many songs, gone within two days of each other.

Sayings are no good to me right now. And I can't believe that I have said useless crap to people, just parroting what others say to those dealing with death. "It gets better with time." Who comes up with this stuff?

The previous winter, a woman had written me a letter about her grief. It was many pages long, and when she handed it to me, she said, "Read it or don't. I needed to write it all out to put my own thoughts to paper." Her mother had died, and what that was bringing up for her was explained clearly on the page. The upheavals in her life, the emotions—the letter was gripping, and I had empathy for her.

But now I understand that I really had no idea what she was talking about. And my response to her, although heartfelt, seems completely clueless in retrospect.

Naturally, prior to May 2019, there had been people whom I cared for deeply who had died. A death affects each of us differently. From the outside, it can look as if someone is isolating themselves, cutting themselves off from the group of mourners who are uniting to deal with their loss. Songs are sometimes the only way I can understand emotionally what is going on, not only with me but with others. Songs are the only way I can decipher the meanings of what I am hearing from voices—be they alive or dead.

Someone told me that her secret code or sign with her pop who passed away had always been butterflies. So she knows when she sees butterflies that her pop is sending her a message. She had a butterfly tattooed covertly behind her ear, under her crop of golden hair. Ever since Mary died, those close to her have been seeing cardinals bold and red because Mary loved her birds. She had her bird feeders and she knew all the birds who came to visit her. I have seen the cardinals only when I am with those who are being visited, being blessed by these messengers. Otherwise, for me, nothing. Surly, I know.

Death is messy, and I am leaking. At least I am holed up in this room trying to contain the mess and possibly write something useful to someone who will enter the death zone today. It's in someone's eyes and in their aura when they are in Death's merciless maw.

I ran into my friend April at the end of May. She has a store on the main street corner in downtown Stuart, Florida, and is usually there. I walked in and saw her in the back of her shop and looked in her eyes and she in mine. She rasped out some words: "I lost my mom . . ."

"Yes, I can see. My heart is with you, April. I lost Mary."

"Yes, I can see. My heart is with you, too."

And there we were: my emptiness hugged her emptiness and we exchanged that explosion of ragged emptiness and both of us walked away filled with more emptiness than before—and somehow that exchange confirmed to me that Death is a club. Everyone will become a member of this club at different times in their life, but April and I have been active members since the middle of spring 2019. We are such regulars that we have our names inscribed on our own deck chairs at Death's Pool Bar. I can find one in any city and in any town, and there my name is: "Bitters With-a-Splash." These clubs are scattered all over the globe, but you have to pay with real pain to keep your membership active.

Currently I am crashing for several days at Death House London. I am close to the nine-hundred-year-old white fortress in the shadow of Tower Bridge, near Traitors' Gate, where inside the ravens reside. There must be at least six ravens there at all times or, so the legend goes, Crown and Country will fall.

There seemed to be far fewer than six of them after all the bombing of London during World War II, but the tradition continues. To make sure they don't stray too far from the tower, each raven has a wing clipped. Other than that, they have a lifestyle similar to the Royals'. They have people coming to see them in droves. They are watched and accounted for and have minders and are attached to a mythic culture greater than themselves. They have perks, so in that way their existence is luxurious. Once in a while, without so much as a backward glance, they have bolted, but usually they have been found either in nearby Greenwich or even at a pub. They can bite if pestered, like most of us, but have been known not only to mourn their own kind but to gather and pay respects to humans they knew who have perished.

Poppy was one of the newer ones, until four baby chicks began hatching on St. George's Day, April 23, 2019.

A raven sat on a railing outside my window for three days back to back in Florida on the Indian River as I was packing to leave—it was the very end of June—a couple of weeks back.

It occurred to me that some children were read lullabies to get to sleep, while Mary would read me Edgar Allan Poe. I was five. When it came to the art of sending me with a talisman into the land of dreams, my mom believed no transportation apparatus would appear by counting sheep. She believed that language and its rhythm could carry the two of us anywhere we needed to go. Poe was her go-to when the sun went down, and as other children were counting sheep and good Christians were off to vespers, her book would open with pages lovingly earmarked. The vicar's wife had her secrets. Mary was a Ravenmaster.

As the moon rises above the old fortress under Tower Bridge, I accept that others are given the medicine they deserve on their grieving journey, whether red birds or butterflies. The gateway to the void is my guide, and I take the unclipped wings of Mary's Raven to understand this time and navigate its darkness. But a song chooses to travel with us to lend us propulsion.

SISTER JANET

Master Shaman
I have come
with my dollie from the shadow side
with a demon and an Englishman
I'm my mother
I'm my son
and nobody else
is slipping the blade in easy
nobody else
is slipping the blade in the marmalade
and
all the angels and all the wizards
black and white
are lighting candles in our hands
can you hear them
touching hands before our eyes
and I can even see sweet Marianne

Sister Janet you have come
from the Woman Clothed with the Sun
your veil is quietly becoming none
Call the Wanderer he has gone
and all those up there

are making it look so easy
with their perfect wings . . .
a wing can cover all sorts of things
and all the angels and all the wizards
black and white
are lighting candles in our hands
can you feel them
touching hands before our eyes
and I can even see sweet Marianne

this again?
Well I think
I could try this
once again

MARK'S FATHER WAS HIS best friend. John, in retrospect, knew his time was nearing its end more than Mark, Mark's mom, Irene, or anyone else. It was December 1998. The cancer surgery had seemed to be a success. He had danced at our wedding the February before, and when I say danced, I mean an amateur Fred Astaire swanning across the floor—pretty impressive moves. After what had seemed a good recovery, considering the seriousness of the cancer, we were preparing for a family Christmas.

It had been a year with very few days off and very little time for family. The tour for *Choirgirl*—my first full band tour, called Plugged—had done what I had hoped it would do artistically. We toured for ten months, going from city to city; bringing some electronics and bandmates to jam with the piano, we had a riot playing music together and being with the crew.

Now it was well-earned family time for me and Mark, so we began the festive season meeting up with John and Irene in London. They were reminding Mark and me of all the characters they had met as publicans since the Second War. The stories ran the gamut from their training years doing pub relief to London pub life in the swinging '60s and early '70s. After that they ran a pub up north in Great Grimsby, which had been one of the most important ports in the North Sea. John told of one day that had begun like any other busy day, when a regular customer from the past showed up hundreds of miles from his stomping ground in Soho, London, to the Rose and Crown in the heart of Grimsby Town. John asked the man how he got there and was told in a lowered voice something like "Had to keep clear of trains and planes and anything obvious, so I hailed a black cab."

John was slightly thrown and asked, "A black cabbie was willing to drive you all the way from London?"

The man clarified: "Well, the chap had to find a call box to get the all-clear from his missus and explained to her that he'd need to be away for at least a few days. But when he told her the price I had offered, which will well cover them for a few months, she asked if her husband could stay longer. So before we head back—once things have settled down a bit and while I lie low here—I've put him up in a room with some spending money over and above his fee, and trust me, he's as 'jolly as a sandboy.' "

John could tell a story and all your problems would just melt away. He brought laughter and the best out of you. And over those magical days and nights during that 1998 holiday season, I found out what everybody else who adored him knew: that being around him always made everybody feel just a bit better about everything. He could make anything all right by putting the right words together, whether in the form of a question or mending your wound by weaving a yarn.

On this particular day, as carolers were underscoring the decorations and with plenty of people watching to be had (the best entertainment on the planet), John suggested the two of us tuck into Soho to pick something out for Mark. After John helped me to choose the present, he asked, "May we go for a little drive and get a cuppa?" He directed the driver where to go, as he knew these streets very well, and expanded on stories of him and Irene as a couple in those wonderful, crazy '60s, encouraging business owners and criminals not to have a violent turf war. He summed up that time by describing a fair but stern Irene famously throwing a Rolling Stone out of their Soho pub.

A dusting of snow had begun when John asked if we could pull over. We both got out of the car and stood under an awning, where he lit up a tailor-made Embassy Number 1 Red. He pointed to the building that had been their pub, took a puff, and said, "It was called the George and Dragon . . . I was George."

Then he got very serious. We were now onto his second smoke.

"You are really going to need to get this right, Tori, because it will possibly help down the line. What I am about to tell you will be a key of sorts for Mark in the coming months."

With his encouragement I retrieved Mark's present from the car. Enveloped now by the flurries, John said, "After I've gone, once Mark has cried all he can cry, show him this train and you tell him exactly what I am about to say: *It's time for you to build this train set and it's no mistake that it is marked with the letters 'GWR.' You know, son, the Great Western Railway is the line that goes to Cornwall and is the same line that had always taken us there since you were a little boy when you, your mum, and I would go to North Cornwall on holiday. And it is the line that will always bring me to you, Mark. Don't forget all the memories made and the ones to be made.*"

After John died in February 1999, a desolate fog descended over the woodlands near the recording studio in Cornwall. Music was being made, and work on my next album, *To Venus and Back*, kept us going. To love someone when they are going through agonizing grief means you know when there are no words that can comfort them.

I tried. We all try to reach the people we love who are in the jaws of grief. For weeks on end there were no words: no touch could reach Mark although he was right next to me; he could have been in China. He was breaking inside but behind an invisible iron mask.

Mary told me to be patient and said whatever I needed emotionally she could send. "Darlin', don't try and draw water from an empty well. That can be dangerous for the both of you and not fair for you to think he can offer you any. Yours is not being replenished from that source, but the music will help, and close your eyes and envision the Indian River. She is tidal and comes in and out every day without fail. I will go to the river myself and drink it in for you, so hold a space to receive it from me, my distraught daughter." She was sending me Mary's Strength. Her wisdom came from a deep understanding, as she had lost both her parents. The passing of her mother in the '70s plunged her into such an emptiness she had been barely alive during that time.

After weeks and weeks of watching Mark go through a relentless oppressive sadness, I heard a voice visit me in the middle of the night. It lured me from sleep and I followed it outside. It was unrecognizable to me. A woman. The tone was one I had not heard before.

She sang to me about 1000 Oceans. About how a person's grief can be so great that their teardrops can form 1000 Oceans, even in a Wasteland. That's how the Muses sometimes work, but they do not work on demand, not for me.

Not feeling confident that Mark would receive this message from this ancient woman, I just played and sang it to him. And that was the beginning of his way back to communicating to me what he was feeling.

As instructed, I took him back to the train set his father had picked out for him and left him alone with it and the message from his father. A GWR model train layout began to be built. It would take a while before Mark could laugh about all the things John said, but the communication line from the George and Dragon in '60s London to present-day Cornwall was up and running, and the old signal boxes seemed to reappear across the landscape even if only Mark and John could see them.

Mary's Raven took my hand again, and we were back with memories past, traveling through our song time machine.

1000 OCEANS

These tears I've cried
I've cried 1000 Oceans
and if it seems I'm floating
in the darkness
well
I can't believe that I would keep
keep you from flying
and I would cry a thousand more
if that's what it takes to sail you home

I'm aware what the rules are
but you know that I will run
you know that I will follow you
over Silbury Hill through the solar field
you know that I will follow you

and if I find you
will you still remember
playing at trains
or does this little blue ball
just fade
away
over Silbury Hill
through the solar field

you know that I will follow you
I'm aware what the rules are
but you know that I will run
you know that I will follow you

these tears I've cried
I've cried 1000 oceans
and if it seems
I'm floating
in the darkness
well
I can't believe
that I would keep
keep you from flying
so I will cry a thousand more
if that's what it takes
to sail you home
sail you home
sail
sail you home

RIGHT: *Dr. Marie Dobyns and Tash*

BELOW: *Jon Evans and Matt Chamberlain, 2009*

ABOVE: *Side Eye*

LEFT: *Kendra Wester and Chelsea Laird Mitchell, 2009 Welcome to England Shoot*

RIGHT: *Neil Gaiman, 2014*
BELOW: *Tash on set*

BELOW: *The crew in Australia, 2014. Back row L to R: Dave "Snakey" Farmer, Marcel van Limbeck, Barry Lee Moe, Mike Lafferty. Middle row L to R: John Witherspoon, TA, Husband, Andy Yates, Miles Barton. Front row L to R: Mindi Pelletier and Glenn Felton*

LEFT: *In the mountains, 2016*
BELOW: *Deep South, 2016*

LEFT: *Little Tennessee Road Trip*
BELOW: *Riding the Ridges—
Smoky Mountains, 2016*

LEFT: *Ed and Mary with
Granddaughter Cody, 2016*

ABOVE: *Cousins—Tash and Kelsey Dobyns, 2018*

TOP RIGHT: *The Studio—Martian Engineering, 2017*

RIGHT: *Harpsichord*

BELOW: *George Peabody Medal, 2019*

RIGHT: *Karen Binns, 2019*

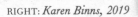

THE RAVENS ARE APPEARING pretty much daily now.

Without having to leave my chair, Mary brings me to Maryland. This is the scene she is showing me: It is September 2004 and she has collapsed in a doctor's office. My sister Marie's office. There is panic, but somehow Marie is able to keep Mary alive until the ambulance arrives. We then see her in the hospital with people shouting "Code Blue!" and all kinds of things are happening that I don't understand, but it looks like Mary is in process of crossing to the other side—whatever that means.

As was later explained to me, Mary's heart had stopped three times that day in 2004. Cardiac arrest. "If you are going to have one of those—much less three in one day," Marie said, "the first one being in a doctor's office, the second in an ambulance, and the third occurring in a full-service hospital, well, that's not bad timing, is it? If you stand a chance of survival."

Later, glued to my broken rocking chair in 2019 during this vision in a sort of seance state, I knew there was a reason Mary had chosen to take us to 2004 with her raven-familiar, but I wasn't quite sure yet what the reason was. We both observed her in that hospital room that September with my father in the corner beside himself with worry and Marie talking to medical staff. Then we saw me visiting her all those years ago.

I was so happy and grateful to see her, talking a mile a minute and going on about miracles. Somehow, in this flashback, Mary had been saved.

Finally I could shut up and look at her. She was troubled. Haunted. We watched us together. She said, *Do you remember when I told you about people who had near-death experiences, and that they reportedly saw a light or heard a voice or received the message that "it was not their time"?* I vaguely remembered her sharing those accounts with me before her own near-death experience. What I noticed now in such a clear way was that she had truly believed in them. Or perhaps *believed* is not quite the word that describes or defines the type of faith Mary had assigned to these phenomenal out-of-body experiences. These accounts—which showed a promise of a type of afterlife—were living, breathing testimony to a part of the Christian faith to which Mary had been fiercely devoted.

We both watched her wait until the two of us were alone. Then she looked directly at me and spoke. "I realize I am fortunate to be alive, but I have to tell someone the truth of what I saw." And it appeared as if the cynical-blasphemous-2004-me allowed a sliver of optimism to inhabit my being. (Anything Mary has shared with me over the years tends to come from the right place. A nonmanipulative place.)

Typically, if I did not see something her way, she did not have the need to change my mind, unless of course I was being destructive or self-destructive, and then she would intervene. With wise energy, armed with unconditional love, she aimed her arrow to root out a poisonous thought or an infected emotion. Mary knew her own mind and would call out and name what she termed her flaws. "But we all have them. Take comfort in that and don't let that fact ruin your day," she would say. "The key is knowing what those flaws are. Not the acting-out behavior that can be a distraction, taking your attention away from the important question: Which one of my flaws has gotten out of the back seat and is now driving the car? When a flaw starts driving the car, your alarm bells need to start ringing. Because that is the perfect opportunity for you to look directly at your flaw and ask it what it needs from you to take its rightful place in the back seat."

She held a space for people to magically own their flaws. (Indeed, she would reward you for this.) She held a space for me to face mine, and I was ready to embrace whatever she was about to tell me of her experience when she was coding.

Mary paused with a defeated shrug. Something of such magnitude reduced to five words: "There was nothing. Just nothing." She had a distressed look.

"Maybe the secret about the afterlife was kept from you because you were always coming back," I riffed.

"Ellen, don't pander. It doesn't become you." Very few people call me Ellen. Most moms, stable ones, earn the right to address you how they want, and it's usually special between you and her. Anything I may have associated with that name is neutralized through my mother's amniotic grace.

She looked me dead in the eye and said, "Ellen, do you understand what I am saying to you?" What *was* she saying to me? For me to hear her I needed to follow her as she took the hand of the Ghost from Memories Past, then opened her other hand for me to take.

THE BEEKEEPER

flaxen hair blowing in the breeze
it is time for the geese to head south
I have come with my mustard seed
I cannot accept that she will be taken
from me

"Do you know who I am" she said
"I'm the one who taps you on the shoulder when it's your time
Don't be afraid I promise she will awake tomorrow somewhere
tomorrow
somewhere"

[—wrap yourself around the Tree of Life and the
    Dance of the Infinity of the Hive—take this message
    to Michael]

I will comb myself into chains
in between the tap dance clan
and your ballerina gang I have come
for The Beekeeper I know you want
you want my Queen
anything but this can you use me instead

ι ι ι

"Do you know who I am" she said
"I'm the one who taps you on the shoulder when it's your time
Do not be afraid I promise that she will awake tomorrow
somewhere tomorrow
somewhere"

in your gown with your breathing mask on
plugged into a heart machine
as if you ever needed one
I must see The Beekeeper I must see
if she'll keep her alive (call engine 49)
I have come with my mustard seed

"Maybe I'm passing you by just passing
you by girl I'm passing you by on my way
on my way I'm just passing you by but don't be confused
One Day I'll be coming for you"
I must see The Beekeeper
I must see The Beekeeper

MARY, HER RAVEN, AND I are watching me find her those many years ago in a motel in Southern Pines, North Carolina.

It had been two months since her Code Blue ordeal and heart surgery. The surgery had gone medically well and she was miraculously on the mend. But she looked ashen.

Michael, her son, my brother, had been killed in an automobile accident several days before.

"Oh, Mom. Oh, God, you really were not well, were you."

No.

We studied the scene together.

This is something I wanted to share with you, Ellen. Grief is something everyone will have to face in their life. No one is totally exempt. And how each person copes or does not cope with it is each person's journey into their own private pain. Let's be honest, some people don't survive it. It should not be a competition. There are no awards for who grieves most sincerely. I was a mother who lost her only son. My faith was shaken. "Why spare me?" was what I asked my God. Only to feel the greatest agony a mother can experience—the loss of her child. There is nothing worse in this world. I am convinced of this.

Mary then recited:

> *"Take thy beak from out my heart, and take thy form from off my door!"*

Quoth the Raven "Nevermore." . . .

"On this home by Horror haunted—tell me truly,
I implore—Is there—is there balm in Gilead?—tell me—
tell me, I implore!"
Quoth the Raven "Nevermore."

She continued, explaining what she had gone through during her grief. *I was having flashbacks to when he was a young boy bringing me flowers that he had picked from our own garden to give me for Mother's Day . . . Purple tulips. Gold Dust. That was Gold Dust. Losing a child is part of my story. It broke me. Yet it made me more compassionate toward anyone who is suffering a loss. But herein lies the reason I brought you here. You can actually do something to work through your grief which I could never do.*

Without really thinking, I asked, "What's that, Mom?"

You can turn it into something that can make all the suffering worth it. And if you never listen to anything I have ever told you, then you really need to heed me right now. . . . Once you finish feeling sorry for yourself that your mother has died, then sharpen your pencil and make this all count. I'm really sorry, Ellen, that you were so traumatized by my stroke. And you and Tori need to pull yourselves together and make what you term "the hell of the last two years" mean something. Anything. It was not either of you, Tori-Ellen, in diapers with your voice stolen from you. Do you understand what I am saying to you?

She started to cry and said, *I loved music and I still love music. You were born practically playing music, and instead of writing songs through all of this and putting what you are feeling into songs, you are* destroying yourself. *You need to get out of this broken rocking chair and stop staring at my ashes. We had a good extra twelve years, didn't we? They happened. They were real. We shared more stories and you wrote a lot of songs about a lot of things. But how are the Muses going to find you if I, your own mother, cannot recognize you anymore? I'm the dead one, not you. Can't I even have* that *to myself?*

Your own daughter, Natashya, is crying out, saying she needs her mother back, and your husband has not seen you for weeks and weeks. And here you are still in this broken rocking chair. So, if nothing is getting through to you, maybe I can. I am reminding you that we are all in your songs. Forever. That is where you can find us. And that is the only thing that may just save you this time. The songs have helped other people to save themselves, and now the songs need to help you save you.

She took my hand and said, *We have just a couple of stops to make before I leave you.*

⟨ ⟨ ⟨

Poppa's funeral. Winter 1973. North Carolina.
Many people of all sorts.
Southern Christian funerals allow grieving with hymns that reflect the doctrine. The belief is in heaven. Heaven was a lifeline for Nanny when Poppa died. They were best friends. Poppa used to sing this song with his beautiful tenor voice in his rocking chair on the porch in Newton, North Carolina, with his pipe smelling of wood cherries burning.

There's a land that is fairer than day
and by faith we can see it afar
for the Father waits over the way
to prepare us a dwelling place there
In the sweet (In the sweet) by and by (by and by)
   we shall meet on that beautiful shore (by and by)
   In the sweet (In the sweet) by and by (by and by)
   we shall meet on that beautiful shore.

You know, dear, Mom said as we were looking in on this time, *you were inconsolable. Do you recall that you spent most of your time at the side of Poppa's grave?*

"I guess. He was my person."

Yes, he was that. And he believed in you. He recognized your music ability and didn't stop talking about the possibilities. He would tell you all his stories and you would sit and listen as he smoked his pipe and rocked in his rocking chair on that porch over there.

"Yes, Mom, I remember that, and I remember crying by his graveside."

You spent a lot of time by his grave.

"I just wanted him back so badly."

Yes, I know, dear one. I wanted him back, too. He loved us both very much. And when you have been given such love and acceptance of just being you—of just being enough for who you truly are—well, why would you ever want to let that go?

I cried. "Mom, I don't want to let go. That's the problem."

Her voice rose: *Don't listen to that song. Listen to your mother.*

Don't let it go. You never have to let it go. You never have to let it go. She touched my heart with her finger. *I'll be right here.*

The Ghost of Memories Past along with Mary, me, and her raven stood back at the funeral home in North Carolina in 1973 as townspeople, great-aunts, uncles, cousins, and their girlfriends in miniskirts, along with some Masons from Poppa's lodge, shared their stories about him.

"Do you remember the time Poppa..." one after the other. Most people called him Poppa. One phrase that found its way into the conversation was about Poppa's belief in Mary and how proud he was of her "academics."

The Memory Ghost took us back to Brevard College in North Carolina, which had held so much promise for her, and then the Ghost showed us Mary getting married to Ed during her freshman year in 1948. Poppa and Nanny did not attend. Mary explained what we were seeing.

They had saved and saved and agreed I would be one of the first in the family to graduate from college and I could have my own future. I would never have to work in the mills, nor would their grandchildren. The cycle was broken. Through their love and personal sacrifice, the stifling cycle of our family had been broken. Education had been the answer to their prayers for a way out. They had believed in me and put everything they had into my schooling. Belief is a powerful force.

"Yes, Mom, it is."

And when we let those down who believe in us it is very upsetting. I don't regret marrying your father. But I never meant to let anyone down.

And she was holding my hand.

THE VICAR'S WIFE

If you find the Vicar's wife
Running through the rain
On her way from Saint James
To Mary's in the field
You'll find she plays guitar
Sometimes with her band
But she plays the bass
Like a Messiah
If you find the Vicar's wife
Staring out to sea
Praying for one more soul
We lose one every week
There she will light a flame
Asking why they've gone
What are we not giving
Giving to the young?
You'll find she plays guitar
Sometimes with her band
But she plays the bass
Like a Messiah
If you find the Vicar's wife
Running through the rain

On her way from Saint James
To Mary's in the field
On her way from Saint James
To Mary's in, Mary's in,
Mary's in the field

MARY LOOKED UP AND SAID, *I really never meant to let* *Poppa and Nanny down.*

"Well, the selfish truth is, Mom, that I had you all to myself as a kid. And if you had been working you would have been very successful and in so much demand that I would not have had all that precious time with you. I would not have been a songwriter. You showed me the stories and you read me the words. And because of that, you showed me the possibilities. And you played me the records. Do you remember when Dad would leave to go to the church in his minister's outfit? You would check to make sure he had pulled out of the driveway."

Mary twinkled and asked, *And then what would we do?*

"You, Mom, would take off your apron, and right in front of my eyes the minister's wife turned into the world's most intelligent DJ and began spinning records. I treasure that more than anything."

Mary smiled. *See, you are recovering your Gold Dust, sweet* *daughter. . . . You hold on to this with both hands. What we have shared* *all these years is not a fantasy. No one, and I mean* no one *can steal this* *from us. Every talk we've had, every walk we have ever taken, every* *song you have sung to me since you were a child—they will live on in our* *hearts and in the songs. Never forget that we all, those of us you wrote* *about, live on in the songs. You can find us all there whenever you need* *us or just want to chat with us. This is your Gold Dust. Never forget this.*

{ { {

February 2019

Mary, her raven, and I are at their house in Florida, called—by everyone who knows my parents—Mary's House.

Mary and I are looking on as Ed, my father, leaves the room with Marie, my sister, and with Mary's caregiver, Olive, to go over something before Marie and I leave for the day.

We both watch as Mary in her wheelchair grabs my hand and starts screaming. She seems to be very alert and awake behind her eyes.

"Mom, Jesus, okay. Okay. I am not sure what you are trying to tell me, but you had a serious stroke."

Mary shakes her head up and down and makes a sort of yip sound for the word "yes." And seems to want more of an explanation.

"The doctors started you on the stroke medicine, TPA, and then they stopped the TPA because some genius idiot decided you were not having a stroke. So they took you off the TPA and sent you to trauma and a different hospital."

From the shadows, the raven, Mary, and I look on as wheelchair-stroke-Mary becomes agitated and starts to scream again while she grabs my jean vest, trying to tell me something.

"Mom, are you trying to tell me what you are going through?" She shakes her head up and down and makes the yip sound again.

Then she looks at me with those eyes that seem the most clear I have seen them since her stroke, and then I begin to speak with her with no one else hearing me.

"Mom, what you have been through is horrible. How you get through each day is truly beyond me. I know that you always said that what happened to Nanny—a horrendous stroke—was your greatest fear. And if that happened to you, you made me promise to not allow people to keep you here on this planet in that state. You have suffered for more than two years now. I believe that you have been willing to sacrifice your quality of life so that we could all adjust to the reality of life without you. And I know Dad has tried to hang on and keep you here. You have given and given and given to all of us. But this is not right. It is not right that you have to suffer. It is cruel. And of all the people I have ever known in this life, you, of all people, did not deserve this mean, devouring fate. And like everything else you have dealt with in your life, you have approached this with as much dignity as anybody ever could wearing a diaper and being trapped in their body as you have been. If I really love you, then I really have to let you continue on your journey without me for a little while. Your whole life you have believed in the power of love and the path of Jesus. Your love, Mom, which is the greatest love I have ever known, will take you to those who need your love next. Thank you for being the best mother I could ever have. You have shown me what Gold Dust truly is."

From the shadows I watch my mom squeeze my hand. Then Mary with her raven speaks to Mary in the wheelchair. "It will soon be time to see Poppa, Nanny, and Michael again. It's time for us to be free."

Mary, her raven, and I leave that scene and end up by a piano. She points to my heart and says, *I'll be right here. Don't let go of the love. The songs will be coming. Trust them with everything you've got. They will sail you home.*

REINDEER KING

Crystal Core
Your mind has been divided from your soul
Now you say you are that stranger on your shore
grief it brings need the naked freeze
caught in the frost
numb unbearable thoughts
your inner need-fire
not lost
no way
not lost

I've just come from the Reindeer King
He says, "Your purity of soul—crystalline"
gotta get you back to you
get you back to you
you gotta get you back to you
get you back to you
You.

Crystal Core
You are at the still point of the turning world
the divide
fearing death desiring life

ϟ ϟ ϟ

Ice you were the one most tender
with the rivers
You the roof
of the waves layer after layer
after
layer

I've just come from the Reindeer King
He says, "your purity of soul—crystalline"
gotta get you back to you
get you back to you
you gotta get you back to you
get you back to you

You know that I would skate
skate all the way
just to hold your hand
to take away your pain
you know that I would skate
from Scandinavia
all the way to the moons
of Jupiter with you

gotta get you back to you
get you back to you

resistance

you gotta get you back to you
get you back to you
you gotta get you back to you
get you back to
You.
I've just come from the Reindeer King

May 2019. A hotel in Baltimore rewriting the commencement
speech I'm about to give at the Peabody Conservatory.
Ripped up pieces of paper are all over the floor around me. Trying
to table the turbulent emotions of grief while tasked with writing a
speech for graduating students is not an easy balancing act—not for
me, anyway.

What happens when all the stages of grief take place in one day?
People have told me that grief can seem like a red ball in a glass box,
the ball growing bigger until it hits the edges of the box. But the
grief I feel is akin to a bull in a box, one that glows red and strains
the parameters of the box and then breaks loose and starts running
around your head and then your room, crashing into any thought
you are having. Exhausting.

Training: I am going to have to pull on and then apply my fifty
years of my music training to get through this week. A week that
honors the hard-won achievements of the music conservatory grad-
uates. It is also a week that honors twenty-five years of RAINN and
the people who dedicate their lives to working on the front lines of
overwhelming, endemic violence.

One of the most important tools I have learned from live performance is the ritual of grounding myself in the place where I am
in that moment. Distracting thoughts and merciless, antagonizing
self-judgments have to be ushered stage right and encouraged to go to

a metaphorical green room. Then my mind begins to clear the daily clutter—even clearing some mental hoarding, if I'm brutally honest.

Then the process of stepping into being a container for the Muses begins. The story of my piano training started in this city—Baltimore. At the age of five I auditioned and was accepted into the Peabody Conservatory prep department to begin formal training in piano and music theory. Whether up the road here in downtown Baltimore at the Peabody itself or across town off Liberty Road, where my father was the pastor for Epworth United Methodist Chapel, I was in training to make music my life's mission. With the intention to serve it and the Muses and never abuse their faith in me as a committed musician to their cause.

The memories visit me in this hotel room by Baltimore's harbor. Fifty years ago, across town on Betlou James Place, every evening my father would come home from his ministerial commitments and sit in his chair and read the paper. He wanted me to play what I was learning for my next piano lesson. He was very much about discipline, which in and of itself is a good quality to develop as an artist. He was also rigidly strict and had very specific ideas about how things should be done. He was very much a "by the Bible" type of minister. He was also very much a "stand up for what you believe in" kind of guy. But if you believed in something different from him, you would certainly have a debate on your hands.

This could work swimmingly well when he was in your corner. Or when he fought the record company that was cheating you. However, if you were the one whose idea he vehemently disagreed with—well, good luck.

Frankly, when I was young working around his energy seemed like the best move. (Teenagers, on the other hand, seem to get off on fighting adults. You get gold stars for it on Teenage Island.) But for a young child, particularly a girl in the mid- to late 1960s, there were not a lot of escape routes. I did develop one skill at this time that has been quite valuable to me over the years. Whether this skill was honed in order not to antagonize my father (if not win his approval), well, this skill really had to work.

Improvisation might not seem like a survival tactic, but it was mine. This is when the skill of turning musical themes I had been hearing over the week into variations on those themes came into being. It was imperative that Dad believe that the Rolling Stones' songs or any other "devil music" was *not* what I was playing—not only because it could pervert a young mind like mine, but he had to believe I was practicing what the Peabody had assigned.

So the variations had to be reimagined into a believable style that could fit in with my approved repertoire. Adversity can work well for the musician and songwriter. It can push you to come to terms with the songwriter you are (and the one you are not).

What I wished another songwriter would have told me years and years ago is that your circumstances make up your story, and no one has exactly your story. It is your very own. You need never envy someone else's life story. Not as a songwriter.

I don't believe anyone's story is boring. Every story has value because it belongs only to you. It is the one true thing that does belong to you and that you can mine for emotional gold. Someone might try to belittle your story or make a joke about it or make you think that your history is worthless because there is a rating system applied to "So what's your story?" But—and I truly mean this— that particular power play can work only if you allow yourself to believe in that nonsense. It's an attack move. I just wish someone had told me that when I was a teenager. And I wish a professional songwriter had reminded me of this when I started listening to people in the music industry about what kind of songs to write. By listening to them, I failed my story. Because of the path I chose, which led to this failure, I had to question my identity as an artist.

That's okay. It's not easy to figure out, and it can be healthy to question.

Some artists seem to know exactly what kind of work they want to create early on in their profession. Others have to find it. If someone had explained to me "Not all artists are brushed in the beginning with their calling as a writer," if someone had said "Different experiences trigger each artist differently," that might have helped me.

If someone had explained that for a certain artist "melancholy" is the guide that turns the key to finding their melody—their artistic path—well, that would have been useful. If they had continued to say "For other songwriters and musicians the effects of melancholy can be debilitating, can be the end of playing music ever again"— this knowledge passed down from writers who had lived through the dark night of their own writing soul would have been valuable to a young, struggling artist.

Perhaps there were musicians and songwriters sharing their well-earned tools of sonic survival, but I was not exposed to them during the building of my music foundation. Therefore there has been a lot of trial and error for me over the years and literally falling off my piano stool and crashing to the ground.

Musicians have talked with me about feeling completely demoralized when it appears that someone in their music course or peer group has discovered their own musical "voice," their own "sound," their own "style." It's not easy being green—I know—but we have to get the green monster back to the circle and encourage artistic growth and not envy. Artists have talked to me about feeling shameful over their envy because the creative magic seems to happen so easily for this person or that person. We as a culture lose some of our future artists before they have discovered their musical identity because they are not aware that it can take years and years to find their own style.

You might be a great player of other people's work, and then you realize that arranging music is your calling. All of this might take some time.

When a musician is talking about quitting their instrument, that is really serious stuff, and those of us from an older generation need to talk them back onto the bridge. Yes, I said back *onto* the bridge.

Some people in music call this bridge "the middle eight" because it has been known to be made up of eight bars. Some writers are great with conjuring choruses; others write great verses; and still others can create bridges. Some can do it all, but sometimes writers just have a knack for one of these sections—verse, chorus, or bridge.

I have a sense of urgency to explore the reality of an artistic crisis through my career. I had to be talked back onto the bridge of songwriting in my mid-twenties. The key to realizing my identity as an artist was failure. My father has asked me to write about this in depth in this book because at ninety years of age he truly believes that failure can have a silver lining. That there, at rock bottom, is where the work of mining your artistic identity can happen.

The important question that restarted me on the path to finding and also rediscovering who I was as an artist, that question from artistic me to personal me was "How did I go from child prodigy to bimbo?" Because that is what a publication called me after the release of *Y Kant Tori Read*. I spent years creating work to answer that question. For a while I lost my way. It can happen. It happened to me. I wish someone had told me that. Just because you have a gift—a musical ability with some notable achievements on your résumé—does not mean that you cannot lose your way and abandon your original pledge to the Muses. You can, and I did. And I survived to tell the tale, but it took work and commitment. The main message here is *not* to quit. And to know that you can be talented and yet a song or a record might not magically fall into your lap. Yes, it might for this artist or that artist. But I have been playing piano for over fifty-three years and am in the process of making my sixteenth studio album, and I can name the songs on one hand that have just fallen right into my lap.

When I would hear an interview with an artist about how quickly an album came together, I wished the radio station would then have played an interview about how tricky making records can be. About how incredibly challenging the whole process is, from the writing of the songs to figuring out the parts for the instruments to the arguments. It is not the norm to have it all figured out when you are eighteen.

Thankfully, I had an entry point into the magic of music by the time I was five and was accepted into the Peabody Conservatory with a repertoire of about two hundred songs. That I could hate music in my twenties would have seemed impossible to me at five. A stab in my heart.

But over the years you can cultivate hate for the art you love. How can that happen? For me it was a combination of factors. Thousands of hours of practicing to gain the facility in my hands as a musician, the sacrifices that have to be made in order to be an able player; then there is trying to make it in the music profession, the rejection of the art you believe in by those in the music industry, while you are working as a music professional . . . dealing with people spilling drinks in the piano and on you as a teenager and misogynist customers changing the lyrics of songs you liked to dirty ditties sung to you by drunk men.

All these moments would eventually become ingredients to sift through in my songs. But at a certain point I knew if I did not get out of the piano bar I would die there, being replaced by some young, mousy, brown-haired girl—younger and less jaded than I—and she would be awarded my job in a hotel piano bar three blocks from the White House, dye her hair red, and get a movie made about her stolen story. Bookers like fresh meat. I knew this by the time I turned twenty-one.

I cultivated hate without realizing it because I talked myself into chasing a specific commercial music vision and took a leaf out of the record business playbook. And then I chased that path all by myself.

I must take responsibility.

What I found is that you must find your own way to your artistic soul.

I wish someone had told me that one artist can hold certain archetypal energies without being devoured by those energies, while another artist may feel as if they are being demonically possessed. One path may really work for one artist but may be mentally catastrophic for another. A drink of emotion can become an elixir for one artist but poison for the other.

I wish that someone had told me of their artistic struggles. Their career earthquakes. And I wish they had stressed that you can find your love for your instrument again and for your artistry after ending up in a funk of resentment. Even after what some musicians call "burnout" or their dreaded "writer's block," we can be showered with creativity's manna and become fertile once again.

In my mid-twenties I was called by the Muses to exorcise my avoidance of my potential artistic self by awakening the pain of my rejections—and all the tumult that comes with that, leading me to uncover my inner darker emotions.

In order to find my way back to the purity of my love for music I had to go find my five-year-old self. Fifty years ago she was down the street from where I was trying to write something supportive to the graduate students of the Peabody. I found her having a whale of a time with a piano across town in the perceptive and underestimated city of Baltimore, diving into the Bones of music structures.

My father told me the other day, along with stories and tears for Mary, that he felt my experience of music failure most notably when

I was kicked out of the Peabody at age eleven and the failure of my first album in the late '80s—that these were great catalysts for artistic change. He wanted more than anything that I expose this. Through big changes like these I was able to regain my love for my instrument, a devotion that is indescribable. She, the piano, has never hurt me in any way. I have betrayed her, and she has forgiven me.

All of this has been brought back from Sister Baltimore and her impeccable memory. She never forgets.

At five years old I had my magic twelve.

The magic twelve for my father would have been the disciples; then, by adding Jesus, you get the power of thirteen. For me the magic twelve were the twelve notes of a scale. By adding the piano to the circle this magic became my magic thirteen. It has been a sorta fairytale.

A SORTA FAIRYTALE

on my way up North
up on the Ventura
I pulled back the hood
and I was talking to you
and I knew then it would be
a lifelong thing but I didn't know
that we
we could break a silver lining

and I'm so sad like a good book
I can't put this day back
a sorta fairytale with you
a sorta fairytale with you

Things you said that day
up on the 101
the girl had come undone
I tried to downplay it
with a bet about us
you said that you'd take it
as long as I could
I could not erase it

} } }

And I'm so sad
like a good book
I can't put this day back
a sorta fairytale with you
a sorta fairytale with you

and I ride alongside
and I rode alongside you then
and I rode alongside
till you lost me there in the open road
and I rode alongside
till the honey spread itself so thin
for me to break your bread
for me to take your word
I had to steal it

And I'm so sad
like a good book
I can't put this day back
a sorta fairytale with you
I could pick back up whenever I feel

down New Mexico way
something 'bout the open road
I knew that he was looking for
some Indian blood and
find a little in you

find a little in me we may be
on this road but we're just
Imposters in this country you know
So we go along and we said
we'd fake it
feel better with Oliver Stone
till I almost smacked him
seemed right that night
I don't know what takes hold
out there in the desert cold
these guys think they must
try and just get over on us

and I'm so sad
like a good book
I can't put this day back
a sorta fairytale with you
a sorta fairytale with you

and I was ridin' by
ridin' alongside
for a while till you lost me
and I was ridin' by
ridin' along till you lost me
till you lost me
in the rear view
you lost me
I said

? ? ?

way up North I took my day
all in all was a pretty nice day
and I put the hood right back where
you could taste heaven perfectly
feel out the summer breeze
didn't know when we'd be back
and I
I don't
didn't think
we'd end up like
like this

WHERE DID IT HAPPEN?

The encounter happened in the kitchen. It happened recently.

It's been several long months since Mary and Beenie passed from this Earth plane. The past many pages have been my journey into this void. Even though pictures of the past were spread out everywhere, I was still having difficulty recollecting experiences with both of them. A picture of each of them would spark a moment in time but then would fade before me quickly.

Through the writing of this book I have had to go through my song history. It was during this process that, as Mary had promised months ago, through waking dreams, I would find memories of those I loved but not on Earth anymore. Instead they were preserved in the songs.

As I began visiting the songs, they began activating all my latent senses. These sonic holograms assisted the songs to act as a time machine. Together the songs themselves and the recordings of them had documented and captured the details of those specific times that had been lying dormant in my mind. When I heard "Crucify," I was transported back thirty years, working with Beenie and Tina Gullickson in the studio. Those two amazing ladies had sung on the demos for *Little Earthquakes* that Eric Rosse and I had been working on. Tina had a tone as clear as a bell. (She still does and has been in the Coral Reefer Band playing with Jimmy Buffett for a long time now.) When it finally did come time in 1990 to record *Little Earthquakes*, the two of them added their talents and spirit sister support to that album.

Beenie not only had a sultry voice but she could do this amazing sound with it that very few people could do. She referred to it as her scream—but I called it "her Janis." Beenie could shoot you to Texas with her Southern Comfort wail.

With each chapter of this book more songs were reviving her and Mary's influence and what they gave to my work and to my life as human muses and as two talented women.

My mind wandered to Ireland, to the hallway of Ballywilliam House. During the recording there of *Boys for Pele*, Beenie shook the rafters singing by the winding staircase as she slayed "In the Springtime of His Voodoo."

The moments kept manifesting: When we were found by Mr. Joel (personal security) wandering the hallway on the floor below our hotel room in Buffalo, where Beenie swore the champers would be fine in the public ice box, tutoring me that people had better manners than to swipe the Cristal, that the magic mushrooms deserved a chilled companion. We bicycled through the stars that night in Buffalo as we had several years before on a patch of grass where we were befriended by some plants north of L.A. back in '89.

I feel a song coming.

Then, out of the blue back in the kitchen, I was overwhelmed by a presence. Jesus, what?

The presence then spoke: *Hi! It's Mom.*

"Mom, where are you?"

I'm with you and you are with me.

"Okay, where's that?"

Well, you can call it the center of the galaxy if you need to call it something. But listen. Just FEEL THIS ENERGY.

And I did.

Darlin', this is the energy you want to infuse in the music in the new songs.

And without saying anything, instantaneously she and I heard my mind say, "But Mom, I have songs I am working on whose bones are grief and anger."

Yes, I know. And those songs come from a place of real emotions you have been feeling. And now, you need to FEEL THIS.

Another blast of Mary Lightning jolted through time and space.

"What is this, Mom?"

It is EVERY thing. Isn't it wonderful?

"But, Mom, when you go away again it will be gone."

I'm right here any time. Free yourself from the trappings of three-dimensional space and time. You know how this energy feels now. You can choose to step into it anytime, anywhere. Persist with this, my dear daughter.

How long we were in the kitchen-anywhere together, I don't know. I forgot to look at the time. But there was something unique about the energy she shared with me. It was immense. In that moment it felt infinite. I am reticent to qualify it any other way, as I want to be clear about what I felt. The word "loving" can be applied because it was brought by Mary and her essence carries that. But it was a different feeling from my usual definition of loving. This surge I felt was not harmful to me; it was an explosive creative power.

tori amos

≀ ≀ ≀

This transcendent experience has pushed me to listen to all the song fragments I have been developing since I finished the album *Native Invader* in 2017. Some hold promise, and others are fodder or attempts that overall don't work. There may be a passage worth salvaging, so I find I have to slog through it or I could miss a piano figure or something else. Self-discipline is an absolute must, and artists have been talking with me about how to apply it and the motivation for it. The reality is that artists can inspire people in all kinds of ways and remind each person they have value. Or the artist will be getting us to see the shocking scope of an issue and how it is affecting us now and paint potential consequences for our near future.

I have had to learn over the years to not lead an artist in a direction I am projecting onto them. My projection might work *not* for this artist but for a different artist. Containment of your opinion is a must if you are going to nurture an artist's development, which might just be in a very fragile state. An artist can be talented but vulnerable and impressionable because of their vulnerability. With the best of intentions a comment such as "Why not lighten this work up a bit?" can send an artist into a negative spiral. I am warning artists that most people *cannot* raise their hand and say, "Your expression, your piece, your song, your art, is not to my taste; in fact I have an aversion to it, but I think it's brilliant." And that means that it is a fact that some people judge something to be good or not good by what they personally like. *Beware of this*, I say to all artists.

A demoralized artist said to me, "They want my work to be more uptempo."

But the truth here is that if an artist is not feeling that way, then the work will tank. Shaming an artist into creating something you want or I want is not serving them—it is trying to get what we want from them. And what we want from them might not be in their creative arsenal. What is key in order for an artist to apply themselves is for them to discover what they have a knack for—what tools they have that work for them. Then the artist can expand the idea and ask themselves, "Do I possess other tools that may be a bit rough but have potential?" The work this artist is creating might not be meant for me or for the person who made a negative comment. The work might not have to be uptempo. What if, for example, the demoralized artist has a gift for writing tragedy or a requiem mass? That artform is not what I would call "up" or snappy. After all, some art is designed to shock us to wake us up. Other artists want to take a different approach. Some write for those in grief. Some want to help us dream again.

My belief at my age now, fifty-six, is that artists are never barren. That is a delusion. I don't mean this with condescension to either those who have been newly creating or to those who have been creating longer than I have. Risks aren't for every artist, but I must admit some do deserve inquiry. I will be open to a notion and test-drive a concept—even a concept to which my instincts are saying, "Do you really have the elements to build and conjure this idea into being? Or are you avoiding the fact that what we've got here is a load of old hot wind and not a magical sonic castle in the air?" Well, it may take investigating to find the answer to that question.

There are some artists I know who are not open to notions. Because a notion is just that: it can be a misguided desire for something to work because I want it to work but it may not have much promise of bearing fruit. Therefore even test-driving some nutty concepts can seem a waste of time.

But in art and creating, I am not risk-averse. I may be in other aspects of my life, but not in music. Not with the piano in the lead by my side and the guiding force in my life. I trust her. More than I trust anything. People can change alliances.

If you take away anything from this book, take this: Instruments do not betray us. We betray them and ourselves and our artist souls. Betrayal—that's all down to us. Why? Why? Why? For commercial success? For fame? Madame Fame is a ruthless mistress to serve. I'm convinced she is a sadist.

You and I have a choice to serve our art over and above anything else. But Fame can be seductive. So we can put practices in place to figure out what our sneaky little inner fame-seekers are up to. We can ask ourselves, "What is my intention for this piece—this project?" Of course I do not take on a project with the intention of failing. But then, what is failure? Something that is not famous with the masses? Just because an artist is famous does not mean they are making great art. It can mean that they have a tremendous magnetism or charisma that has contributed greatly to their success. And those skills must be acknowledged, though they are different from the skills needed for making important art.

My interest at this time in our history is to find and share every arrow in my arsenal to confront any issue an artist at this time may be facing, that which is keeping them from allowing themselves to create. Yes, sometimes the artist is lacking in ideas. But an artist as barren? That is not a notion I would apply to my artistic process; it is a delusion. Farmers and gardeners apply the word "barren" to soil or a crop, and whether it has happened because of extreme weather or they need to fallow that portion of land and plant in another, "barren" in this context makes sense. That isn't to say that the farmer and the gardener are not facing a setback or even a devastating loss, but for them the word "barren" is not a delusion. But because "barren" is one of those words that for the longest time, for thousands of years, has been associated with a woman's value—with being incapable of producing offspring—this concept contains an unjust finality in it.

Artists don't have "limited" access to the universal creative force. Unlike a gardener and farmer who may have a certain number of acres they can work while the land recovers, we do not have those constraints. We just don't. The real estate of the universal creative force is infinite. We must act defiantly against the delusion of being creatively barren, because that is a delusion that, when applied to the artist, can infect and spread. People trade in delusions all the time; therefore, an artist can buy into this delusion. But there is another way forward.

A song can help me to set ground rules. Different artists have their way of doing this. For me, there are conditions that have to be put into place. The spirit world must be respected, as well as the human world.

The intention of creating must be made clear. There is no need for fear if you are clear. There are some artists who choose not to set conditions. They say they are open to anything—and yes, some of them create with anything. Whether assisted by drugs or alcohol spirits or not. But if you do not set your boundaries in a clear way, outside forces can invade your space and there can be real consequences to this conjuring. My experience is that the spirit world does respond to intentions and conditions and boundaries. However, people on average can be less respectful than spirits. So as far as setting a boundary goes, some humans will still test your authority—even your authority over your own being.

The song "Dātura" is forbidding anyone with a destructive intent from entering her garden. At the same time, she is inviting the plants to safety and a place to flourish and share their knowledge with those who are receptive.

DĀTURA

Hey
get out of my garden
Hey You
get out of my garden

passion vine
texas sage
indigo spires salvia
confederate jasmine
royal cape plumbago
arica palm
pygmy date palm
snow-on-the-mountain
pink powderpuff
Dātura
crinum lily
st. christopher's lily
silver dollar eucalyptus
white african iris
katie's charm ruella
variegated shell ginger
florida coontie
Dātura

ming fern
sword fern
dianella
walking iris
chocolate cherries allamanda
awabuki viburnum

natal plum
black magic ti
mexican bush sage
gumbo limbo
golden shrimp
belize sage
senna
weeping sabicu
golden shower tree
bird of paradise
come in
variegated shell ginger
Dātura
lonicera
red velvet costus
xanadu philodendron
snow queen hibiscus
frangipani
bleeding heart

resistance

persian shield
cat's whiskers
royal palm
sweet alyssum
petting bamboo
orange jasmine
clitoria blue pea
downy jasmine
Dātura

is there room in my heart
for you to follow your heart
and not need more blood
from the tip of your star
is there room in my heart
for you to follow your heart and not need more blood
from the tip of your star
is there room in my heart for you to follow your heart
and not need more blood from the tip of your star

Hey
get out of my garden

Dividing Canaan
Dividing Canaan
Dividing Canaan
piece by piece

tori amos

Dividing Canaan
piece by piece
Dividing Canaan
oh let me see
Dividing Canaan
Dātura

THERE IS ANOTHER WAY through and past the delusion of "barren." People who are addicted to power can live on the same street or attend the same school as us or even play on the world stage. They can weaponize the thought of being creatively barren in order to debilitate the artist. They target artists specifically because they know that artists have the ability to reach the public in ways no one else can. They know this. And what they do not want is to be called out or held to account or revealed to be the manipulator they are and that they are a person aroused by the possibility of absolute power. That is a naked truth. And they do not want it exposed in pictures or songs or poems or articles or books or film or through dance. So when the propaganda spreads about "writer's block" or "an artistically barren portion of time," especially when it comes to women, this poisonous propaganda gets magnified. And then it can drown out reason and become a probable eventuality. Although it is merely a projection, unfortunately it can become an imposed self-fulfilling prophecy.

How we see the creative process can determine if our thoughts are either working with us to make art or working against us to keep us from the potential art we so want to make. Thoughts are such powerful inhibitors or helpful conspirators that we have to look at what they are up to and then we can put certain practices in place. I consciously choose to see my process as cyclical. If I were to write songs all the time, when would I be gathering new seed concepts to plant in my creative garden? It is only fair and important to stress that the gathering of new ideas is not done by luck or by the roll of dice. And yes, sometimes the artist needs to rest, although some tell me they can't sleep. I understand this, and sometimes I actually do envy people who can sleep. So sometimes the gathering phase is a mixture of taking in information and hibernating—when the secret to sleep has been discovered.

Sometimes I literally draw, or I should say scribble, my process on paper to concretize my process out of ether and onto something tangible. When I draw a circle, *hibernating/healing* may be one of the points on the circle. Another point on the circle may be the *taking-in phase*, through reading or observation, and this will invariably take me to a place of commitment and patience for the research that will lead to the *seed gathering* for the project. This process is building the foundation for eventual *output or giving out*, a third point on the circle. This is where the song comes together and the sonic garden begins to reveal herself. Which, of course, gives me energy and endorphins and spins the circle, which generates more energy. The fourth point on the circle would be the alignment of *taking in and giving out*, which work together like breathing. This is when the artist becomes a container, receiving the inspiration and sharing it all at the same time. The most obvious example of this in my art is during live performance.

All these processes are part of my developmental cycle of a project.

All four points on the circle can happen in one day when we're on tour.

To say there are not frustrations or setbacks traveling around the circle would be untrue. And honestly, I then have to take the time to drill down on the details and the effects each component is having on the overall piece. And only then can a different but informed approach or change be made. I might have to change direction to break through an impasse with myself or with a team member. The paradox of using the word "change" in that context is that a vital part of making music is the art of effortlessly going from "change to change." That is the quest. That is the magic. One "change" can sneak into another with notes being added to a chord that then morph into another "change" or "chord." Shorthand-speak in a studio will be "So what's the change in bar 72?" Changes are chords made up of notes and the building blocks of music.

In the context of music, changes are not a thing to be gotten rid of. (Unlike *You need to change your behavior, young lady* or *I need a change in my life to get out of this oppressive existence*.) Sometimes a musician will ask, "Can we change this horrible change?" The composer will usually say, "That's an intentional horrible change and it underscores the story," or the composer or arranger will say, "Of course that's not meant to be there. Yikes—can you believe that? It's gotta be the copyist's fault." And everybody laughs and gets on with playing the piece. (We can all write a stinker of a change that sounds workable on a piano or a keyboard until you hear it coming back at you by the instrument for which it was designed—and then *Crash!!!* Best to giggle at yourself and change it after all.)

Changes in music are working together even if they are conjuring purposeful tension. Together they aim to bring transcendence.

A change/chord is not a lesser version of another change/chord. In my experience every single combination of notes has value and has a role. They might not be heard as frequently or be as popular as the "ear-pleasing" combinations, but each one can be utilized. It's not a competition to see who can use the weirder chords the wisest, although some of us will be drawn to the strange or what is thought of as discordant. In this context, the idea of "making changes" is not about making it better when you leave one chord and go to the next; it's about a rotation similar to the planets and how they affect one another.

Music theory people can help explain the language far better than I can. There are people I know who write great songs who have not studied much theory. I am finding music theory to be quite useful these days and not tedious. (My teenage self found it a snore.) But like most things, music theory is a language, and if you are engaged with it, it can become a world in itself, an adventure.

Hopefully this book will be a companion and a source of support to artists and those who adore them. My intention has been to be honest about the journey of the artist. An artist's journey is not for the faint of heart. Every word in this book aims to be supportive of artists and to vanquish the demonic thought-form of creative paralysis.

Mother Nature is an immense reflection of seasons and cycles and inspires my artistic process. She is our spiritual Mother and she needs all of her artists to step forward, to find their own unique voice and create in these tumultuous times. Yes. We must Out-Create destruction. It is the only way. Destruction can possess and it must be Out-Created by us. Together. We will climb out of the belly of the beast together.

CLIMB

"climb over the church wall" he said
"you can feed the koi in the pond
climb over the church wall in your Sunday dress
be sure to feed the koi in the pond"
It's a long long climb going back in time

all of me wants to believe
that the angels will find me Saint Veronica
all of me wants to believe
that somehow you will save me Saint Veronica

he said "kneel before your judges in reverence
your penance for the woman you'll become
you knew if you talked there'd be a consequence
your sentence for the woman you'll become"
ten days of hell in Satan's cell

all of me wants to believe
that the angels will find me Saint Veronica
all of me wants to believe
that somehow you will save me Saint Veronica

dream of dimensions
then cross through the veil to them

wrap yourself in linen holding Jesus close
calling Saint Veronica

"climb out of the belly of the beast" she said
"become a witness out of the abyss
the temple of the soul will have to heal the flesh
only when you're whole can you forgive
but it's a long long climb"
it's a
long
long
climb

acknowledgments

FIRST, I WOULD LIKE to thank my editor, Rakesh Satyal, for believing I could do this. I will miss our endless conversations. Thanks also to John Witherspoon, my manager, for going through this book with me line by line in our final edit stage. To Husband, who said he wouldn't buy the book unless there were pictures in it. To Tash for her insight and patience for listening to every draft of this for the last two years.

To Dr. Marie Dobyns for accuracy. Other family information was provided by Tim and Beth Amos, Karen and Keith James, Jane and Steve Broddle, and Aunty Joyce. To those who have encouraged and supported me through the writing of this book, my nieces and nephews and their partners, Cody and Marco, Casey and Rachel, Kit and Sarah, Cory and Angela, and last but never least, Kelsey Dobyns.

To Kavita Kaul for making me recite my lyrics to her. The cheerleading squad of Mike and Kathleen Dugan, John Bobb and his gang. Mary Ellen Bobb and Al and Gail Tacconelli.

To Neil Gaiman for encouragement. For the vote of confidence, thanks to Super Debs, Lara Thorne, Adam Spry, and Christine Espley. To my ride or die Karen Binns. To the treasured friendship of Nancy Shanks (Beenie). To all of those who have been supportive of me in my career (there have been so many), you know who you are.

To my father for his tenacity all these years and for never letting me off the hook. To the wonderful women who cared for Mother Mary and are also caring for Ed now, Olive Glenn, Yvonne Edwards, Janice Douglas, and Magon Wilson.

To all of you who have written letters and given me insight for almost thirty years now.

To Carole Kinzel at CAA and Mike Dewdney at ITB in London for sending me on all those crazy miles of touring over the last three decades. To my ever-faithful crews and fellow troubadours and collaborators. To my literary agent at CAA, Mollie Glick. To Susan Tucker at Rehmann Robson for all the support. The Seattle sweat lodge sisters. My spirit sisters and brothers whose prayers have kept me going through this. And, as always, Curtis Kekahbah.

With all my gratitude to the Muses, Song Beings, and the Piano.

~ ~ ~

Photo credits and acknowledgments (and gratitude) to: Billy Reckert, Alison Supple Evans, Chelsea Laird Mitchell, Jenni Clark Keyes, Eric Keyes, John Witherspoon, Tori Amos, Jenn Daranyi, Karen Binns, Mark Hawley, Dr. Marie Dobyns, Kavita Kaul, Barry Lee Moe, Mindi Pelletier.

references

Below is a list of sources that provided particular guidance during the composition of this book.

Pages 18–22:

The United States Air Force / airforce.com

Col. James H. Kyle and John Robert Eidson, *The Guts to Try: The Untold Story of the Iran Hostage Rescue Mission by the On-Scene Desert Commander* (Ballantine Books, 1995)

Mark Bowden, "The Desert One Debacle," *The Atlantic* (May 2006)

Page 83:

Rape, Abuse and Incest National Network / RAINN.org

Pages 92–99:

United Nations Population Fund / UNFPA.org

World Health Organization / who.int

Centers for Disease Control and Prevention / cdc.gov

Page 107:

Emma Lazarus, "The New Colossus"

Pages 213–14:

Edgar Allan Poe, "The Raven"

about the author

TORI AMOS IS a Grammy-nominated singer-songwriter, pianist, composer, and, with Ann Powers, the *New York Times* bestselling author of *Tori Amos: Piece by Piece*. She has released fifteen studio albums, including her latest, *Native Invader*, in 2017.